How To Clean Your Underwear In Africa

by Matthew Hulland

ISBN-13: 978-1492397717
ISBN-10:1492397717

DEDICATION

To all the amazing people I met along the way and to the people that make the projects. Thank you for the memories and keep dreaming big.

For project donations;

www.matthulland.com

Contents

1. The Begining

The Beginning

The idea was simple, for years I have wanted to travel in Africa, see what voluntary work involved and make that career change that I keep talking about. So, like any other sane adult I decided to quit my job, run away to Africa and try to do something different upon my return. In the UK we see the appeal videos that try to make us give our money to various charities, all the children looking sad and in tears, but I have never been sure of where that money goes. There are a lot of people involved in these charities and I am sure that they get paid somehow but also I am sure that they do a lot of good and change people's lives in ways we couldn't imagine over here. I wanted to see for myself what Africa was like and see if I could make a difference on a small budget. With no experience of travelling alone I decided that the South East of Africa was a good choice as it is comparatively stable.

Having decided to go, my first task was to track down a volunteer company to help set myself up on a project in Africa. This alone was a bit of a challenge as the volunteer market seems to be quite a competitive one, there were so many options. One thing I didn't like were all the ones where you have to raise a minimum sponsorship, I didn't feel it was right to ask my friends and family to give me money for a donation to pay for a trip I wanted to do for myself. With those out of the way the selection was getting narrowed down. Some of the companies offer packages where you pay one price which covers everything, flight, transfers, accommodation, meals etc. I also didn't want to do this as it seemed more like an all-inclusive activity package rather than getting into the local community. I am not saying that is what it would be like but just in my head. Whilst searching I came across a company called Original Volunteers. This one seemed like it was more what I was looking for. Basically you pay them a subscription fee and a one off donation of £50, I'll fill you in with where that goes later, and that is it. You let them know when you will be in the project town, they book your spot in the accommodation and put you in touch with the project co-ordinator and the rest of it is up to you. This suited me perfectly as I wanted to do some travelling around Africa as well as the volunteer work so I signed up to working in Tanzania and handed my notice in to quit my job.

Research

Research and planning were two things that were a lot harder than I thought they'd be. I bought a couple of guide books but found them pretty useless, so my main resource was the internet. I find guide books tend to be great when you get where you are going but not so much for the planning stage (shame I forgot mine and left it at home). When I was trying to research my trip all I could find to answer any questions I had were online forums. They are good but it is always a pain when you have to write a question, hope someone finds it and replies to you. Information can take a long time to come by. Also the other hard bit about the forums is you get different advice from different people and it is so hard to find all the information you need in just one place. If anything, after researching on line I was more scared than if I hadn't done it. Most of what you find is stories of when things go wrong, people have been robbed or hurt. It's normal because if you have a bad experience of something you want to tell everyone but if it was good you are less likely to pass your story on. Think of when you go to a restaurant - if you have a good experience you tell people it was good, maybe a specific dish which was outstanding but if you have a bad time you tell people the story from the beginning to the end about how bad it was and with extra detail.

Most of my questions tended to be about visas and bus timetables. You can get a lot of information about visas from the embassy websites of the particular country you are visiting but it is still quite confusing. However, as this part of Africa is a bit behind the times in the IT department none of the bus stations or companies have websites. Or no

3

stations have timetables so it is really hard to truly plan. This can be quite frustrating from a Western view point but once you have been there and experienced an African bus station you'll understand. They are crazy, crazy places I think it is hard enough for a local to know what is going on let alone tourists and they can be very intimidating. However the fact that I am sat here writing this is a testament to them working . . . somehow. I think the reason advice is so hard to come by is that it is different for everyone and things are always changing (being run on African time doesn't help). The one time I found a timetable (TAZARA train) and I arrived a little early to be safe the train turned up 9 hours late. As with most things, people have good experiences and people have bad experiences, if you are smart and alert you should be fine, have minimal problems and enjoy those experiences.

So on with the story;

2. Day 1 - Hungover

Day 1, Heathrow Airport, London

Note to self, no matter how much you believe you'll be alright DO NOT arrange leaving drinks for the day before you fly. To put it poetically I have felt like crap since I woke up this morning and am just about coming around as I sit in the departure lounge at Heathrow airport. The combined feelings of having a severe cold, being hung-over and being very nervous about a mad trip I am about to embark on to Africa is not a nice mix. The final few things I should have managed to do before I left didn't get completed but at least I did get to "enjoy" about 7 episodes of Come Dine With Me on the television while lazing on the couch nursing the hangover. At least I am very glad I packed last night!

So far not much to report, lunch at Carluccio's for an emotional goodbye to the future wife and a car journey that made me want to bring my lunch back up again. As always when traveling to the airport with my Dad we arrived in plenty of time. Check in was all a bit hazy but I did manage to find some cheap sunglasses in Boots having managed to leave mine at home, along with my flip flops and $100 that was given to me as a leaving gift from the guys at work. More evidence of why you do not fly after a night out. I did manage to find some flip flops in the airport but at £40 I decided not to buy. Before I left, my doctor advised me to make sure you wear flip flops in the shower at all times to stop these funny little parasites crawling up through your skin and attacking you. I'm not sure what the parasites do, but I will assume it's bad so I better hope to find some in Nairobi pretty quickly otherwise I may have to start smelling funky as a different option.

I guess that's it for day 1. I am feeling pretty light-headed, probably the mix of beer (last nights and the one I just had in Strada for £5.30), anti-congestion pills, doxycyclin or whatever it is and a few other things, hope it will at least let me sleep! I still don't think the fact that in 24hrs I will be alone in Nairobi has really set in yet. Maybe the tired, confused feeling isn't so bad after all, if it wasn't that then I'd probably be pretty scared.

Oh, and by the way, I hate flying..........

Learnt on Day 1;

1) Do not drink too much the day before you fly.
2) Do make sure you are packed at least a day before you fly.
3) Spend your time before your flight checking you have all of the essentials like flip-flops and sunglasses, not recovering on the couch watching Come Dine With Me. Not that there's anything wrong with Come dine With Me, there are other TV options available, but it's not really a good idea to lie down watching it when you should be packing your flip-flops.
4) Take plenty of money, airports are expensive.

3. Day 2 - Arrival

Day 2, just about, Dubai Airport

Landed in Dubai fine, enjoyable flight, 2 hours sleep and watched The Avengers. I seem to have now lost my voice, which is nice, also managed to lose my phone and my wallet at the security check. It's quite hard to blame anyone but myself. When changing planes you have to go through another mini security check when you have to get everything x-rayed again. I took my bag off and put my wallet and phone in the little box to go through the x-ray, walked through the scanner fine, picked my bag up the other side and went on my way. A few minutes later I fancied a drink...oh, no wallet! I ran back to the checkpoint but there was no sign of the wallet or phone anywhere. On the plus side I still had all my cash and my passport and three hours to find the wallet and phone. The advice from Mum to keep money in separate places and not all in your wallet now seems like the best I ever had! First place to start looking was with the police, who were no help; from the police to the customer services to lost and found, back to the police, and then to the security again. By now I had covered the airport about three times. Bear in mind I had lost my voice so communicating to foreign people is even harder than it should be. It has been quite an experience; no-one seemed to care too much about helping. After two hours checking everywhere possible and desperate for a coffee I thought about cancelling the cards, luckily the airport has free Wi-Fi. A quick bank balance check later, nothing had been spent. I was ready to cancel but I thought I'd just check Facebook first and thank god for Facebook. I had a message from Kinga (fiancée at home) saying some nice man has found my wallet and managed to get it to my departure gate. Turns out he found the wallet and the phone and managed to call Kinga from the phone to tell her he had my stuff and he would hand it in to my departure gate. So I wandered and was re-united with phone and wallet. Sadly all the money in there has gone but it was only £10, cards are all in place and driving licence so I am happy with that. I just need to keep an eye on my accounts in case the cards have been cloned but more importantly I could buy a coffee! Upon finding my phone the mysterious South African who found it managed to call Kinga, this makes me wonder...if I had a pin number set up on my phone so no-one else could use it, it would have been impossible for him to call Kinga and I wouldn't have got my phone or wallet back. Phone locks and pin numbers are great, but sometimes...who knows...on to Nairobi.

Day 2, still

I really am my father's child; on the way from Heathrow to Dubai I managed to smother myself in sweet chilli sauce. Next leg, Dubai to Nairobi, I covered myself in chocolate, the old man would be proud. I May be running out of clothes sooner than expected - only two more hours before landing in Kenya. Oh, and apparently if I fall asleep sitting upright I tend to dribble on myself.

Day 2, final entry, made it to Nairobi, Kenya

Wow, I'm not going to lie, it is scary, a lot scarier than I would have thought. I checked into my hotel and decided to go for a walk to find the train station. I walked around for about 35 minutes and just couldn't find it. The sun started to set and I thought it'd be best to head back to the safety of the hotel as I don't know anything about Nairobi.

The fact that almost every shop and hotel has a guard outside brandishing AK-47s makes me think it's not the safest place to be alone at night. Most of the people you walk past on the street seem fine but every now and again you get a look and it just makes you feel uncomfortable. Maybe it's just me creating those looks as it's so different from home and my first experience as a minority, I haven't seen another white person yet, I am so far out of my comfort zone.

Anyway, I landed. My first concern was visas and how that all works, it's really easy. You just follow everyone off the plane to the visa desk, pay $50 and move on through. There are a few options on visas so make sure you get the correct one. I had a simple tourist visa, you can get a transit visa if you are travelling straight through and out of Kenya which I believe is $30 or a multiple entry visa for $70. If you plan to leave Kenya and re-enter make sure you get this one otherwise you will end up paying the full $50 again upon re-entry. Bear this in mind if you are thinking of doing a gorilla trek in Uganda. The current price list and restrictions for visas can be found on the Kenyan embassy page but you do not need to arrange and buy one before you leave as it is possible to get all the simple visas when you land. Just remember to take lots of US dollars. After clearing immigration I collected my bag, changed some money (easy to do) and wandered out of the airport. As soon as I walked out I was accosted by about 15 people all shouting "Taxi Taxi" - very intimidating. I didn't want to get in the first one I came across as I wanted a bit of time to gather my thoughts so I wandered around for a bit but every other step there was someone else wanting you to get into their taxi. The first man to approach me grabbed my arm and tried to drag me to a car, he was pointing to the car park, pointing at his car. It was away from the main taxi area and looked pretty beat up so I decided not to trust him and moved on, in fact I was quite wary about most of them so I made sure I got into one with an official sticker on it. It dawned on me later that I had no idea what an official sticker should look like but I guess the thought was there. After selecting my taxi and nearly causing a fight between the guy I chose and the first man that approached me (apparently if you tell them you are not after a taxi and then get in someone else's they take offence) I was on my way to downtown Nairobi. The ride from the airport turned out to be very good - nice guy got me here in one piece although the driving is pretty manic. At one point a mini bus pulled off the road and just drove up the path honking his horn to clear people out of his way rather than wait in line. It seems that you make your own rules here!

I am staying at The New Oakwood Hotel, seems good so far, Wi-Fi's not working though which is a real bummer as that was one of the reasons I booked here. It is right in the middle of the city which is good but quite loud and unfortunately the TV only has one working channel, a crappy music channel, probably going to be an early night. Good news; whilst I didn't find the train station I found a place to buy some flip flops. They cost me 229 shillings (about £1.50) much better than the £40 option and now I can shower myself with confidence.

That's about it for now, going to check the hotel bar and maybe grab some food, my first official Kenyan meal, fingers crossed! There's a Hilton around the corner as well so maybe that's an option if it's no good here - don't feel comfortable yet to go into any of the locals bars. Tomorrow is still up in the air, the original plan was to get the train tomorrow evening to Mombasa but I was meant to book the ticket today, sadly I got lost and didn't find the train station. I will probably head over there tomorrow during the day to try and buy a ticket, if I can't then maybe it's another day here then get the bus. I'm pretty terrified of both options, maybe time to fly home!!

Learnt on day 2;
1) Never leave your wallet behind at an airport scanner when you have lost your voice. In fact don't leave it behind at all.
2) Think carefully about your phone pin code as if you lose it and it is found by an honest person they cannot help you. I picked up a cheap pay as you go phone before I left England so if, or when, I lost it I wouldn't mind too much and by having to top up you have complete control over spending.
3) Take extra tissues or napkins for the plane ride as you will spill food on yourself.
4) Visas can be bought at the airport, just check on the Kenyan Embassy website which one will be best for you and don't forget about the multiple entry option, could save you a lot of money.
5) Don't get into the first taxi, take a moment to suss out the situation.
6) Ensure you get a price from the taxi driver before you get into the car and barter, barter, barter, you can get the price down as there are lots of taxis wanting your business.

4. Day 3 - Nairobi

Day 3, beginning

Went to sleep last night at 10pm so feeling pretty good this morning, voice is returning, by tomorrow I think I'll be back to full voice which will be nice.
Breakfast was interesting, mango or passion fruit juice, no orange. And curried vegetables with naan bread, not what I would normally choose but enjoyable all the same. Last night I just had a meal in the small hotel restaurant. It was enjoyable and my first taste of ulaki, a traditional Kenyan food. I had it with my first Kenyan beer, Tusker, crisp, light and clean, nicely chilled, it was a perfect finish to a stressful day. If all African beers are of a similar quality then they will be enjoyable. On the news they were reporting a couple of shoot-outs in Mombasa between a separatist movement and the Government which has got me a little more nervous but I think it'll be fine. They managed to arrest the leader of the movement and his wife and although it's a bit north of where I'll be in Mombasa (if I get there) depends on if I can find the train station tomorrow!

In the newspaper;
There was a man arrested and sentenced to 18 months in prison for beating his wife with the back of a machete, injuring her quite badly. The next story is how a man stole two sacks of Irish potatoes and went to prison for two years. Doesn't seem quite fair to me!

Anyway, I'm off out.

Day 3, entry 2

Well the unknown turned into a great day. What to say? Breakfast was ok, kind of strange taking a big slug of mango juice when you're expecting it to be orange but I just about got through it in one piece!!

Anyways, the fun starts once outside. I thought it'd be a good day to do a bit of exploring around Nairobi but I didn't really know where I was. I asked the receptionist in the hotel and he told me of a tourist information place where I may be able to get a map of the city, so off I trotted. The problem with Nairobi seems to be everyone wants to "offer" you something, be it a whistle then "taxi taxi" or just a quick chat and then ask for money. This time I was fine as I knew where I was heading. As I was walking towards the building, after three shouts of "taxi", a guy approached me, right outside the tourist office, and asked me what I was after. I explained that I just wanted a map and walked straight past him into the tourist office. Once in there the lady told me they had no maps, but told me somewhere that would have maps and pointed to the guy who I ignored outside as someone who could show me where. I thought it strange that a place advertising tourist information had no maps but given that the hotel I stayed in pointed me this way I trusted the place and wandered off with the guy from outside and learnt his name was Charles.

I was suspicious of Charles and his motivations. Being Western, and given all the research I had done before I came here, I am taught to be suspicious of any local offering things. I am very happy to say my day with Charles was fantastic. We wandered off to go to the place that the lady recommended to get a map whilst engaging in small talk. Once there I was offered various safaris and day trips but after saying I just wanted a map so I could get to the train station and book my ticket to Mombasa they duly obliged. At this point I was still suspicious of Charles but I was told he would be happy to walk me down to the station so I agreed. We walked and talked about Kenya, living in Kenya and growing up here. It was really interesting and he took me right to the ticket office at the station. Most of the journey there was fine but from about 200m way from the train station you have to walk through the bus station. I have never seen anything like it. Before I go any further I feel I have to note I am writing this while sat on the train, I have neighbours (who we'll get to later) but I can't work out if the noise I hear is that of the train straining or them. Headphones in either way and turn the volume up!

Anyway, buses...I have no idea how to explain it. There must have been about 100 buses all in a small space, probably about the size of a football pitch, fighting for passengers and offering deals. Every bus has a man outside just shouting noise. I can only assume he is telling you where the bus is going, it must make some sense to the locals. The buses themselves are tiny, they are like VW camper vans, no bigger but with the amount of people getting on they must be like a Tardis inside! I am hoping the bus from Mombasa to Dar Es Salaam is not going to be anything like this otherwise I have some quick learning to do as it made no sense to me. Amazing to see but no idea what was going on. Once I have taken a bus I hope it will make a little more sense, otherwise who knows where I'll end up?

Inside the train station I managed to buy my ticket, first class, and we walked back to the hotel. There are three different options in buying a train ticket, first, second or third class. The third class is simply a seat booked, second class gets you a sleeping cabin shared with 5 other people and first get you a sleeper shared with one other and all your bedding and meals. The difference in price between second and first is about £5 and it means you share your cabin with one other as opposed to five others so I figured it was £5 well spent (third was never really an option for my first overnight train trip). While booking my ticket there was a European girl travelling alone, I'd guess early twenties. She booked a 3rd class single and seemed happy to do so so I'd assume it's fine for a cheap ride. After booking the ticket Charles walked me back and then asked what else I had planned for the day to which I honestly replied nothing. He offered me the same trips as the other man in the tourist office, including the city tour where you drive around seeing stuff. Having got the taxi yesterday and spent 10mins in traffic without even moving I did not fancy this so I asked if we could do a tour on foot and all of a sudden Charles become my personal tour guide. We walked...a lot...and talked, it was great. We started off by wandering to the National Museum of Kenya where I learnt a lot about the Kenyan history, how they gained independence in 1963, the Mau Mau's and about the fights in 1992 for two party elections and of course about the history of humanity. So many of the most important fossils in human evolution were found here. At the same site they had the snake pit, like a mini snake zoo. I came face to face with vipers, spitting cobras and black mambas, well, face to face with a sheet of glass in between. All in all a great place to visit. The museum also has an art gallery with a temporary exhibition of children's art from around the world and some of it is fantastic, all about peace for Kenya and the world. I really hope they grow up and still hold faith in that and follow those dreams.

There is still so much to write but I have been a while now and I need to get to sleep, it is 1:30am, breakfast I believe is served at 7, so time to try and get some shut eye. I have had to gaffer tape the armrest that keeps falling on my head (thanks Mum for the tape) and the train is moving and shaking like a 50s rocker rolling on an ice cream machine, but I will try to pass out. I think the Kenya Ken will help, but more about that tomorrow, for now, goodnight. xxx

Learnt on day 3;

1) Don't leave your guide book at home, or at least take your own map.
2) Bus stations are crazy . . . Good luck!
3) National museum of Kenya is a good visit.
4) The little extra dollar for first class is worth it.
5) Not everyone who approaches you in the street is a crook, guides are a great way to see the local area and learn as you go, I guess you just have to use your intuition to choose the right one or go to http://www.trekkingkenya.com to track down Charles.

5. Day 4 - Kenya Ken

Day 4, early

Woken up at 6:30ish this morning by a rather harshly rung bell right outside my room indicating it's time for breakfast. Luckily whoever my room-mate was meant to be didn't show up for the train so I had a private room, albeit interlocking with another couple. Breakfast was hardly inspiring, a small glass of mango juice, bit of fruit and fried eggs with beans and some kind of a sausage I think. The coffee pouring was quite amusing, the train during breakfast was kind of like crossing the English Channel on a bouncy castle, a little bit up and down. I have no idea how but the waiting staff managed to get most of the coffee into the cup but once it was there it didn't want to stay! Flying off all over the place, amazingly I managed to stay quite clean but I was sat opposite a Spanish couple from Mallorca who struggled. By the end of breakfast the majority of their coffee was in their laps. All in all given the fact we were on a train the breakfast was quite tasty and very entertaining.

So far the train journey has been great, not too much sleep and still feeling a little rough after exploring Kenya Ken last night but fascinating. Outside is an amazing expanse of rough looking nothing interspersed with random settlements of local people. There are plenty of young kids outside begging at the window, I want to take pictures but I have nothing to give them so I am trying to restrain myself. I think for the next train ride I will buy some stuff to hand out, every time the train stops you hear this pitter patter of little feet outside running up and down, trying to get in, almost like a spoof horror movie. Anyway, the train is due into Mombasa at 9am, currently it's 9:08 and there's no sign

17

of a city yet. Could be due to the one hour delay when we were meant to pass a cargo train. Unfortunately the cargo train had broken down so they sent our engine off to move the cargo train to a place we could pass, gave us back our engine and we were on our way again. Quite a few cheers and waves as our drivers went past pulling the cargo train out of the way!

So back to yesterday, I believe I was in the museum. After we left we walked back towards the city centre again. We passed a place that was known locally as Devil's Corner, the site of a lot of killings during the fight for independence. Once independence was granted the new government donated the land to religion and Devil's Corner is now the site of three large churches and a synagogue, nothing like building on the devils own land, I love the idea. From there we headed to Uhuru (freedom) park. Here is where you get a great view of Nairobi and is where all the Prime Ministers and Presidents must be sworn in and take an oath in a very public way. It used to be that they would take an oath in private so no-one really knew what they were promising to do! Also the site of Pope John Paul the 12th's mass back in 1980, as a Christian Charles was very proud to have been there. This got us talking about religion, which as you can imagine took quite a bit of time and got us through to lunch. I asked to go somewhere very traditional for lunch and I wasn't disappointed. I had chicken soup and he had fish both served with ulaki, it is a local maize dough like product. This stuff you could say was A-maize-ing (sorry) - no cutlery or napkins and I was eating soup, bound to be messy but great fun. Being polite I waited for Charles to start, really I just wanted to know how the hell I was meant to eat this stuff. The ulaki is basically a lump, kind of like edible play dough, tastes a bit like play dough too, but this meant it was easily mouldable. So, the way to do it is rip off some ulaki, mould it into a rough spoon shape, dip it in your soup and stick the whole thing in your mouth, amazing and awesome, I would be happy to eat every meal like that. The only downside is I think I had a very skinny chicken so I managed to eat most of the meat off the bone but couldn't really get to parts of it because of my front tooth.

I had a minor setback about 1 month before I left for my trip. Having booked and paid for everything and handing my notice in at work I picked up my stick for my usual Saturday hockey game. I have played hockey for my local club on and off for 15 years. I have never broken a bone or even had a minor injury and I and found myself thinking about this in the car on the way to the game. As always shit happens. At some point during that game I went in for a tackle, at the same time the guy I was tackling swung his stick and caught me full force right in the face. I was lucky in a way as it just caught my tooth as opposed to shattering my lower jaw but it did manage to take my front left tooth clean out and severely dislodge the one to the left of that. Luckily our club chairman was on the sideline, he recommended that I put it back in, he is a doctor, so I gave the tooth in my hand a little rinse and stuck it straight back in. Well, not completely straight, but it's in there. A quick trip to A & E followed by 7 trips to the dentist and double root canal it was a busy month before I left. Turns out putting it back in is the best thing you can do, they say if the tooth goes back in within an hour you have a 90% chance of keeping the tooth, if it is out for longer you have a 90% chance the tooth will have to stay out. Bear in mind I am not in any way qualified to give medical advice so what you do when your tooth falls out is entirely up to you and I accept no responsibility for what may happen.

Although I was struggling with the skinny chicken, Charles was having no problems with the fish, reduced to a pile of bones, I have never seen someone eat every part from the tail all the way through and seemingly saving sucking the head dry of the brains and eyeballs till last! Pretty impressive, guess I'm just a big softie! After lunch we went our separate ways but I did ask him if he would mind helping me with my stuff to the train station, to which he agreed, a great help.

In the afternoon I did my first bit of haggling, buying a shirt for 1000 shillings instead of 1200, still a bit of a "white man's price" as they refer to it but I think I did ok, I'm sure I'll have plenty of more time to practise. After my first Africa shopping experience I sat in the hotel for a bit, doing some studying like a good boy and learning some Swahili, they keep telling me it's an easy language but I disagree. So far I have learnt;

Habiri - a way of saying hello how are you
Asante - Thank you
Choo kiko wapi - Where's the toilet?

I don't think I'll need anything else!

After a couple of hours in the hotel bar, relaxing and studying I met up with Charles again and he walked me to the train station, helping with my bags. Once there we said our goodbyes and on I got the train. There was a little confusion as in the UK when you buy your ticket that's your ticket. Here it is a little different, you seem to buy a ticket for a ticket. When you get to the station you have to go back to the ticket office and exchange your ticket that you bought earlier for a boarding pass which has seat numbers and stuff on it, but don't worry too much about those kind of things as everything is always late you'll have plenty of time to work stuff out.

 As I mentioned earlier, the cabins are inter-locking and I am in a cabin next to an Aussie called John with who he refers to as his "tour guide". Now I'm not sure how much he is paying for his tour but he seems to get plenty of extras. At least his guide is better looking than Charles, half his age, better looking and female. John was a fun guy, seems to have done a fair amount of travelling around Africa at various times with various "guides" so knows some stuff. We were rung to dinner which we had with a local Mombasan lady who was also lovely so we all sat around after dinner, shared a bottle of wine, couple of beers and some Kenyan Ken. This is a local spirit distilled from sugar cane, had no real flavour to it. I imagine it's what the locals drink in their downtime for a bit of a kick, probably add some mango juice to it to liven it up a bit, still, got to try the local products. The main local beer is called Tusker, tastes good right now, I'd imagine in England it wouldn't be quite the same. Dinner times are great on the train as you get sat in groups with people you don't know and it is the best opportunity to get to know others, especially over a couple of the local drinks. When you are at dinner you have to leave your cabin, which also means leaving your stuff behind. I had read a lot about thefts on trains before I came out and was under the impression that it is more a case of what gets stolen rather than if anything will go missing. John had bought some cable ties with him which was a great idea as you can use them to fasten your toggles together. Its not really high security but it will make it hard for the opportunist to quickly dip into your backpack. Also just make sure you have a smaller bag to keep anything valuable like phone, wallet, camera etc. with you at all times, just common sense really. I am happy to say that getting back after dinner nothing had been stolen.

I guess that's it for now, we're moving again and the landscape has changed from fiery red desert, red like the Devon soil, to sand and palm trees so I think we are getting close. Time to tidy and get ready to go, Mombasa here I come, don't kidnap me!

Day 4 - Mombasa, Kenya

The train arrived in Mombasa at 10:40ish, not as bad as I thought it would be. I got off, said my goodbyes to John and his guide and hopped in a cab to the hotel, New Palm Hotel for two nights. Accommodation pretty shabby, TV crap, Wi-Fi seems to not be working (on-going theme) but it does have A/C. Even after all those bad things this place is quite nice, open plan first floor is quite different. Just watching some poor King Arthur movie before I pop out to try and work out how I'm going to get the bus to Dar Es Salaam on Saturday. I hope it is a nice coach because some of the ones I have been seeing quite frankly frighten me.

Day 4 - continued

So I have my bus booked to Dar, quite painless in the end, I popped into an agent she told me it was going to be $240. After a mild panic attack I realised she was quoting me for a flight! After explaining that was a bit much and she let me know where to go to book a bus ticket so I waved down a tuk tuk and it whizzed me off to the bus station where I managed to book my ticket for Saturday (at 5:30am). I will have to spend one night in Dar Es Salaam, not sure where yet, and then on to Iringa (base of the project in Tanzania) the next day. I decided to sort out my ticket as soon as I could just to put my mind at ease. I am still really unsure about the bus stations and seeing the one outside the Nairobi train station made it even worse. As it turns out it was very simple. There is an area of the city where all the different busses are, you will need to find out which company drives the route you need and just go to their base to buy your ticket. It is possible to buy it on the day but bus travel is very popular and they often leave very early in the morning so I would recommend getting it as soon as you can. This also gives you the opportunity to choose your seat which can be a nice bonus. To find out the company you need you can just ask at your hotel, hostel or as I did in a local travel agent, get them to write it down with the address and just hop in a tuk tuk and they will take you there. In general the tuk tuk drivers seem to be quite honest with their pricing and charge you the same for every trip but it is still always best to confirm a price before you get in. If you are in a different city with no tuk tuks and need to get a cab make sure you negotiate a fair a price first or they will try to rip you off. It always helps if you know roughly how far it is you have to go, sometimes as it will turn out you were so close could have walked. When booking my bus ticket I was once again asked if I would like to upgrade to VIP class which I have never known on a bus before so I agreed just to check out what it was like.

Bus ticket sorted I now have two days to enjoy Mombasa. I've really enjoyed riding the tuk tuks but apart from that there is not much to do in the city. I went to for a walk around the old town and that was pretty scary. It started

well, nice old buildings, sea view, but then the street
disappeared and it was really tiny alleys with loads of
people just sitting around. I felt quite unnerved, didn't help
when I saw a guy with a Somalia (pirates) top on. I was lost,
so I just kept on walking with my head down trying to look
like I knew where I was going. Every corner I turned just
seemed to be getting me deeper and deeper into the dirty,
smelly back streets of Mombasa being stared at by locals
from every angle who knew full well I was lost. After about
20mins of being trapped in a maze of tiny streets I came to
somewhere I recognised and felt a massive sigh of relief as I
was back out in the main streets. Upon reflection I am sure I
was never in any danger and could have asked any of those
people for help and I would have been fine, but at the time
it was very uncomfortable as I am still new to Africa! After I
regained my composure I wandered down to Fort Jesus, an
old Portuguese fort that was made in the shape of a human
to represent Jesus. After wandering around I assume that it
wasn't a very good fort as it was taken from the Portuguese
by the Arabs, then from the Arabs by the British - it has
changed hands more often than a library book. Whilst
walking down to the fort I was approached by some random
guy who was very frustrating as he just walked next to me
the whole way talking at me. I wanted to tell him to piss off
but sadly I am too polite. It's so hard when they come up
and talk to you so politely to simply ignore them, although
that's what I should do. When inside the fort there was
another guy but this time an accredited tour guide offering
to show me around. I had already paid 800 shillings to get in
and he wanted more money to show me around. I should
have just politely declined but my head was all fuzzy still
from the old town and from the man outside so I just went
with the flow. He showed me around and told me a few
things about the fort before leaving me in a museum and

asking for money to feed his family. He didn't really do much to earn it and it cost me another 550 shillings, wish I'd shown myself around. I am learning this is the way they do it in here, they have to live on their wits which means you have to keep yours about you.

Having felt cheated I came back to the hotel to sulk. I left briefly to get some food but otherwise just been sulking in my room and trying to sort out the rest of my trip. Not too sure what to do tomorrow as I need a cheap day, maybe a day to do plenty of revision. In summary, I'll probably not bother coming back to Mombasa.

Learnt on day 4;

1) Buy your tickets for onward travel as early as possible.
2) Eating breakfast and drinking coffee on a bouncy train is very entertaining.
3) Tuk tuks are awesome.
4) Try to have something to secure your backpack (zip ties or at worse string can be used) when you do have to leave it behind and ensure you keep valuables on you at all times.
5) Old town Mombasa is quite intimidating on your own, if you want to feel safer get a guide or go with others.
6) Fort Jesus is worth seeing by chose your guide wisely and try to get a price first – I didn't.
7) People approaching you on streets normally want money, your choice if you give it or not but I think giving encourages begging. It is a really hard one as these people have nothing else and I am sure given the choice they would rather not be having to approach strangers and ask them for money but

unfortunately that is where life takes them. Just remember you will hear a lot of sad stories, many of them are just that, stories and you won't be able to help everyone with handouts.

8)   You will spend more money than you think!

9)   Culture shock is a bitch, that is what I am putting my fear for the first few days down to.

6. Day 5 - Cleaning Pants

Day 5 - Mombasa, still

So much for cheap day, as soon as I left the hotel I got accosted by another tour guide, this time though I negotiated a good deal to go out to Haller Park where there are lots of animals so it worked out well in the end. The day started with the worst breakfast ever, there was just about enough stuff there to scrape together a sausage sandwich which has kept me going until now. The upside was that they had run out of Nescafe sachets so I got to enjoy a proper coffee rather than the instant stuff they usually give out for breakfast. With no plans for my day at this point and not feeling too optimistic about another day in Mombasa I sat in my room watching Barca vs. Madrid followed by some horrible Chevy Chase movie whilst washing some clothes. Hand washing pants in a small hand sink with no plug is a right pain in the backside. Note to self; next time travelling take a universal plug! Once my pants were on my little home made washing line with bungee cords (thanks Mum) I decided to man up and venture out.

Having smelt all my clothes and knowing what I still have to come I decided to see if I could buy a shirt and also to wander up to the massive tusks that are a monument from the Queen's visit in 1952 so I'd at least have a picture of Mombasa. As I was walking I was approached by another tour guide who wanted to sell me some trips as usual. I'm not sure why they always pick me, maybe I stand out, I thought I'd bought clothes to blend in, must be the way I walk or something. Anyway, after telling him I wasn't interested he mentioned Haller Park, it is a small animal park which is popular but about 7-8 kms away so I didn't

27

think I'd get to go. We haggled on price and I got it at $35 including transport and ticketed entry so I agreed to meet up again later. I had been doing some research and quite fancied the park, more of a zoo so after getting a good price I was happy to go. Before we went to the park he offered to show me around the town a little so we went for a walk, he showed me a few temples and mosques and another Freedom park with a lot of mango trees full of bats which was pretty cool. He dropped me off at a supermarket so I could pick up a few snacks for my trip tomorrow - 5am start. The supermarket was interesting, a lot of strange things but a lot of familiar too, Heinz, Coke etc. Afer finishing my shopping I relaxed in the hotel for a little before meeting Teddy (tour guide) and off we went to the park. I will say again, the driving is amazing, how you can drive with all those mini buses and tuk tuks around is beyond me. Somehow we made it one piece, passing the market on the way. That place looked crazy, I was recommended by someone I should check it out but I don't think I'd do it on my own!

Haller Park was great, got to feed giraffes, play with a 140yr old tortoise, watch hippos being fed and them trying to chase off the monkeys from stealing their food but the highlight was the crocodile feeding. I have seen many a crocodile in zoos but they never do much, here I got to see them feeding. One of them must have been between 10-12 feet long and at least about two or three feet wide. When he was fed I was being polite and I let a few ladies in front of me so they could get closer while I was trying to hold my camera above them to get a good picture. While I was playing around with aperture settings or something like that there was this massive sound like a hollow tree falling followed by a whole load of panicking, screaming women running away. I am not going to lie, I was scared about what may have just happened. It turns out it was just the sound of the croc's jaws closing loudly and it scared the ladies so much they tried to stampede me! Death by stampede of large, middle aged African ladies. When I thought of the many ways I could die on this trip that one was definitely not on the list! With them out the way I was at least able to get a good picture. He snapped again and the noise was fantastic, so loud, and then he got the meat and off he went. The other part of the park that was interesting was while we were waiting for the hippos to be fed. I could hear a rustling in the bushes all around - it was the sound of the monkeys waiting to steal the hippo food. As fun as it was I had never thought about one thing.....monkey toilet time! Unfortunately for the lady next to me, nor had she. All of a sudden a localised rain shower hit her right on the head, luckily we both moved from that tree before the hail storm followed! As much as I love monkeys I forgot that when nature calls they are often up high and gravity will always win. After a quick good-bye to the 140yr old tortoise, who had moved about 7 feet in two hours, we were on our way.

For the journey back we hopped in one of the local mini buses (known as a matatu), now these are crazy. More so than the tuk tuks and they're quite crazy. They are all about the size of the old VW campers, just like the ones I saw in Nairobi, and they cram, I mean cram people in there. At one point I think we had about 19 people in the eight seats available but great fun. Bombing along the Mombasa highway, horn honking every turn and loud music pumping out, this is Africa I thought, finally. I wish I knew the city better and wasn't scared of everyone (my English paranoia) as I would love to ride more of these. You do need to know where you're going though, I have a problem with this as I don't, and nowhere has a map! Between the tuk tuks and the matatus I am starting to change my mind and think I could enjoy this city given more time to learn it, which I don't have as I move on tomorrow. Did I mention 5am?

That is about it for now; I am currently sat in a cafe writing this. Cafe Aroma is the name and it is great, lovely atmosphere and great food. I was asking the taxi driver on the way from the station what Mombasan food I should have and he recommended a biriyani, and I have to say it was fantastic. Also in a day full of highlights, Cafe Aroma sells sausage rolls so I had to have one. Bear in mind, I am a bit of a pro in the sausage roll department but I have to say this was very good, lovely pastry. The only downside of my dining experience is that the drink has arrived at my table without the cap on it. I noticed earlier on in my trip that wherever you eat they will always bring your drink to the table in a bottle with the cap on and open it at your table. I ask Charles about this back in Nairobi and he explained that drugging of drinks is a big problem in Kenya so they have to open it at the table to prove that it hasn't been tampered with. The drugging here is more common on men and more associated with robberies rather than sexual assault so it is men that need to be wary more so than the women. As mentioned my drink has come to the table with no top on it but I didn't even think about it until half way through at which point I also realised that everyone was staring at me. I thought of what Charles had told me and feel a little concerned that I had been drugged, not much I can do about it right now so I guess I'll wait and see what happens. Time to pack up and head back to the hotel before any drugs kick in!

Day 5 - Mombasa 1 last time

Well I am still alive, un-robbed so I guess I haven't been drugged, shame really as I could do with the drugs to get me to sleep. It is amazingly hot with the a/c broken, sweating my pants off and sooooo much noise outside, I know earlier I said I loved the tuk tuks, right now they can go to hell. Oh and I realised why every one was looking at me, not anything to do with drugs but I had managed to sit directly under a television, not a good idea if you already feel like you stand out.

Things learnt on Day 5;
1)   Take a universal sink plug if you want to keep your underpants kind of clean.
2)   And something to use as a washing line, bungee cords work well.
3)   Haller park is a good trip out.
4)   If you are brave enough and get the chance, ride a matutu.
5)   Cafe Aroma in Nkrumah Road, Mombasa close to Fort Jesus, does a mean biriyani and is simply a nice place. If you are feeling slightly out of place and think people are looking at you then don't sit under the television.

7. Day 6 - Another Hotel

Day 6 - Dar Es Salaam, Tanzania

So here I am sat in another crappy hotel room but at least I have a TV which has the Premier League on it! I have just returned from dinner where I had a lovely beef curry with two beers for the costly total of £6!
So I don't know if I had mentioned but my day started very early today, had to get up for the bus at 4:45am which I somehow managed having had no sleep. Got packed and left the hotel for my final tuk tuk ride, gonna miss those guys, to hop on the bus.

The bus left on time and I had a lovely seat right behind the driver for what was quite a crazy ride. Mombasa city is on an island and apparently the quickest way off is using the ferry. For some reason the bus stopped way before the ferry terminal and everyone started getting off which was a little strange. I asked if I had to get off as well but I was told to stay. I assume this is something to do with having paid for a more expensive ticket. So there we were, the bus driver, two others and I waiting on the bus when the ferry drifted in from the other side and I've never seen anything like it. Must have been about 4-500 people all waiting for the gates to open and then GO, they were all sprinting somewhere, I didn't see where but I have never seemed a ferry empty so quickly. I am struggling to keep my eyes open at the moment so I think I am going to finish this entry here. Tomorrow I am back on the road again, I have a bus to Iringa at 7am to go and meet up at the project. I am very excited to be in one place for a few weeks, just have a 10hr bus journey to get through first! I have no idea what to expect from here forward, well to be fair I didn't really know what to expect from the beginning, but we will see what happens. Goodnight again.

8. Days 7-10 - How to Overtake in Africa

Day 7 - Project Iringa, Tanzania

Ummmm, it's late, about to go to sleep, I have no sleeping bag, I'm sweaty, I've lost my beloved Torquay United fleece, but I'm still alive. A lot to catch up on, to be continued when I am more awake! Zzzzzzzz

Day 10 – Project, Iringa, Tanzania

So much to catch up on, I have been too busy lately to keep this diary up to date but will try to write about it all. I last left it on the ferry crossing with hundreds of people sprinting and jockeying for position off the ferry to be front of the queue for wherever they were going. The first ferry emptied pretty quickly then a second one docked whilst we were trying to drive on board so in true African style with hundreds of people running in front of him the bus driver just beeped his horn and ploughed on through the crowd. I must have heard three or four people bounce off the bus, but I guess that's their fault!

After a bit of trouble getting the bus onto the ferry we were free to continue our journey the other side. All the people who disappeared returned, got back on the bus and we were on our way. Until now being at the front seemed great but the downside is I get a great view of the driving and to say the driver was mental would be a bit of an understatement. He had about eight different horns and used every one of them a lot! Overtaking around blind corners, I think we spent more time on the wrong side of the road than we did ours, and I would not want to be a cyclist. It seems you are the impala of the road, just there to get picked on by others. If you are cycling and you hear a horn you better get out of the way because the bus is coming through. The amount of cyclists diving off the side of the road was quite something. So when in this situation I did the one thing I am good at, closed my eyes and fell asleep. I believe everyone has a superpower somewhere deep inside of them, mine is my ability to sleep anywhere, anytime, anyplace, great for scary bus journeys you want to be over quickly.

I was woken up about two hours later with a little slap from my neighbour on the bus to inform me we had reached the border crossing. Feeling rather groggy I collected my passport, joined everyone else in getting off the bus and watched the bus drive away. I was a little nervous of how this would all work as I had never crossed a border on foot before so just followed the crowd. First of all you have to line up to get your Kenya exit stamp, after a few simple questions that was done. After that you walk across no-man's land, quite eerie as it was so quiet and just desert before you walk through a big fence then you have to get your Tanzania entry stamp. A man asked to see my yellow fever certificate, I had forgotten about that so luckily it was in my hand luggage. He didn't even check it, just wanted to see a yellow piece of paper. Once I got my stamp, I was in and found the bus 200 yards up the road and off we go again, easy as that. What was quite scary was at the side of the road there's a little wooden shack dishing out yellow fever injections for $30 in case you don't have your certificate, I am so glad that I didn't have to go in there! Stood at the border are lots of people trying to buy and sell currency, it is recommended not to use them but I had to as I had no Tanzanian shillings. I knew it was going to be a bad rate but I only changed a little bit so I could buy a drink and some snacks along the journey. The man changing the money was polite and I had no problems, just make sure you are roughly aware of the exchange rate and negotiate.

All this commotion did a good job of waking me up so I had the opportunity to really enjoy the driving. Rather than sit there like a scared little puppy, given my advantage of the view I had I studied and there are patterns. What I managed to work out was:

1) Beep your horn if you want to overtake.
2) The lorry/car in front will indicate left if the path is clear or right if not.
3) You rely on the person in front telling the truth.
4) If you are behind something and the car coming the other way flashes at you then it means the coast is clear to overtake.

Knowing that there is a system made me feel a bit better and I was able to relax and enjoyed the rest of the trip. In total, with stops, the journey took about 15hrs. Knowing this I was very careful to limit my water intake so I did not need a pee all journey, one of my big recommendations when travelling around here on buses. The stops were quite fun though with loads of people sprinting to the bus trying to sell you drinks and corn on the cobs, all kinds of treats. I didn't mind the drinks but some of the food looked a bit untrustworthy.

Once we had arrived in Dar Es Salaam my first task was to buy a ticket for Iringa. We got off the bus somewhere in Dar and I found someone to ask where to get a ticket. Rather than tell me he decided to walk me, I was taken through loads of worrying back roads before we finally found somewhere to buy the ticket. The man then walked me back to the bus drop off and I got a taxi to the hotel. I thought that I was close to the hotel as I purposely booked one near the bus station so when I asked how much the taxi would be I was quite surprised when he said 20,000 shillings, I was expecting 5000! So I started to negotiate and much to the driver's disgust he agreed 12,000. I still thought that was a lot for a five minute taxi ride. As it turns out I was nowhere near the bus station or the hotel so the ride took about 30mins. I had been dropped off in the middle of Dar rather than the main bus station which is on the outskirts. Feeling a little guilty about the negotiations I decided to pay him the full 20,000. It's funny, when you are coming out here you are told to negotiate everything and even when you do you will still get ripped off. I cannot argue with that but sometimes you find yourself haggling over the equivalent of 50p and it just feels a bit silly as 50p to me isn't much, but to your average African trying to make a living selling on the streets that is worth masses more. Sometimes it's better to just suck up the white man price and let them earn their money. Anyway, I made it to the hotel by the bus station in time for dinner and snoozing but I have already mentioned that. Overall day six was a pretty good day.

The next morning it was time to catch the bus to Iringa. After another awful breakfast I left the hotel and got a tuk tuk to the bus station. Given the amount of touts outside I asked the driver to take me all the way inside to where my bus (Sunry) would depart from. I had heard stories about the bus station in Dar and it didn't disappoint. It was so big with people everywhere, a very confusing place to be. Outside the main entrance there are touts all over the place trying to get you to buy tickets from them. They can't be

37

trusted which is why I always like to have my ticket before I get to the bus station. When inside we walked around but could not find my bus - my tuk tuk driver spoke to a couple of people and told me it was not yet there but wait here and it will come. To be fair, I wasn't 100% sure he knew what he was talking about but with no other option I just sat and waited. Various people approached me, trying to sell me stuff but they were harmless. One guy came up to ask me which bus I was waiting for so I told him but he then told me it was cancelled but he could get me a ticket for another one! Yeah right sounds like a scam to me, good try mister. So I sat and I waited...and waited...and waited. I was starting to get a bit worried so I went to try and find someone to help, the problem was who to trust. I managed about three laps of the bus station and I thought about going to the ticket office but it meant wandering through 100s of touts so I kept walking. I thought it would be a good idea to ask someone who was working there but it was really hard as no one really has a uniform. I did find one man who was organising the boarding of another bus and asked him - he pointed me in the right direction. Turns out the bus was cancelled! Luckily my ticket was valid on another bus which I managed to track down. I boarded the bus and off we went. I still can't work out if the original man was telling the truth or trying to rip me off.

Anyway, once on the bus (that was meant to leave at 9:30am) I was sitting in a nice window seat. I was reading before I came out here that the bus basically leaves when it is full, now I know it to be true. By 10am I still had my window seat but had a rather large lady next to me. By 10:30 they came round and made us sit in our assigned seats. That meant I had to switch with large lady into the aisle seat and at 11am we finally pulled away and all was good, apart from being the most uncomfortable bus I have ever been (but on at least I had some space). The driving was pretty erratic but I am used to it by now. About 20mins into our journey we pulled over after being chased down by a honking motorbike and another man got on, rather large again. I think he must have missed it and chased it down which to be fair is pretty awesome, but missing a bus that was already an hour and a half late is pretty special. So he got on and was assigned a seat right next to me, so now I am next to two large people and with myself having a rather large bum it left me with enough room on the seat for one cheek. With a 12 hour bus journey ahead I knew it wasn't going to be comfortable. Mustering all my strength I decided early on to use my super sleep power and managed to pass out for the first three hours. I then woke up, well most of me, my floating cheek was never quite the same. The rest of the journey was pretty hot, sweaty, squished and hellish but 10hrs later I arrived in Iringa. The views were good, especially during one mountain pass with sheer drops, even knowing the system I will never believe overtaking around a blind bend with 20-30m drops off the edge is ever a safe option, but we made it. Once I arrived in Iringa someone arrived within 15mins to take me to the voulunteer house.

I had no idea what to expect when I got to the house, and even thought I may be on my own, but I was greeted by six others who seemed pretty nice right away. The house itself was a bit of a mess, blocked sink full of skanky water, cigarette ash all over the floor, just a bit of a filth hole really. If you bear in mind that is my opinion (and my fiancée will tell you about my dubious relationship with clean and tidy) then you will understand it was really filthy. I didn't even mention the kitchen.

Luckily for me two of the volunteers were leaving the next day so I was instantly involved in a leaving party which was a great way to meet people quickly and try the local drink of choice - Konyagi! It was a pretty fun night, few beers, bit of food and home to bed ready to start work tomorrow. I guess that brings everything up to date for now. I have just had my last planned shave of the trip, thought I should try and look presentable for my first few days at least. Time to start volunteering!

Things learnt on this part;

1) Don't stand in front of a bus at an African ferry crossing.

2) Never cycle along a main bus route.

3) If you have to exchange money at a border make sure you negotiate and don't change too much.

4) Get your jabs as you don't want to end up in a roadside jab-shack.

5) If you are staying near Dar Es Salaam bus station I can recommend the Rombo Greenview Hotel.

6) If you are using Dar bus station get your taxi/tuk tuk driver to take you inside to avoid all the touts out front. If you need to buy your ticket there ask the driver to help you.

7) Once inside the bus station if you need help look to ask the people loading the busses but beware some of them will tell you to get on their bus

and charge you for another ticket so stay smart.

9. Day 19 and The Project

Day 19 - A lot to catch up on!!!

Well, I am now just over a week in, as you can tell by the lack of entries I am way behind and have a lot to catch up on, time to list the days:

Project Day (PD) 1 - After sorting out our visas ($200) we started off by visiting an orphanage in Upendo, it was pretty mad. We went and watched some other volunteers teaching a class about body parts. The classroom was so tiny with just a few desks and a chalkboard and the kids were from all different ages seemingly from 10-17yrs old. There is no teaching structure or lesson records so no way to know what the kids do or don't know. The most shocking thing to me was that they didn't even know how old they were or where they are from. Most of these kids were abandoned by their parents often left at the side of the road or just placed on a bus and left there, but even in their dire situation they are still so full of life and fun to be with. One kid especially, called Ali, is a great little guy. I would guess him to be 10 or 11 but so full of charisma and life - he's the kind of kid you see and know it's a shame he is not going to get the chance to fulfil his potential. I really hope someone can find him and give him the chance he needs. When we were done at the orphanage we met up for lunch at a place called Safari (see separate entry for info about places I eat at) which was pretty good. It did feel a little strange having been at the orphanage and then going to lunch in a place that looked like a mini paradise, being served by the locals. It was from one extreme to the other, I

41

was wondering what the kids would make of it being sat there, getting your food served and enjoying the luxury and wondered if any of the rest of the group felt the same.

In the afternoon I went with a couple of other guys to a construction project in a local village. We were told to meet for the bus at 2:30pm and when I turned up I was pretty damn worried! The bus looked about 50 years old, hasn't seen a safety inspection in its life and about 20 people too many crammed in it. An amazing sight was watching the spare wheel go on. It is kept on top of the bus and was carried up there by one man balancing it on his head climbing a ladder on the side of the bus. Now bear in mind the wheel's the size of a tractor's (the big rear one, not the crappy little front one) it was pretty damn impressive. After a bit of a palaver trying to get into our seats we managed to pull away. After various stops, bumpy dirt roads with no suspension and giving a football away to random kids in a random village we arrived three hours later. We were introduced to our hosts for the night and shown where we were sleeping in a local village house and then shown to the project we'd be working at.

The project itself is great; they are building a school for the local girls as currently they have to walk about 10kms to school. The issue with this is that in this part of African culture the girls do all of the chores, cooking, cleaning, fetching water, that kind of thing. To get to school the girls in the village have to wake up around 4:30am in time to do everything they need to do in time to get to school. Upon their return they are expected to help around the house leaving them shattered and not able to do home work. Due to these demands it is very rare for the girls to pass a primary education and move onto secondary school. The idea of the project is to create an all girls' school that will help relieve the problem and give the girls a better chance. We went to the building site where the work has already been started, there is the class room building up but still needing a roof. The foundation stones were all around the trenches dug to put them in for the accommodation block, which was our job in the morning. As well as the buildings they have dug a well for water, planted mango trees and started work on a chicken hatchery to help sustain the school in the future. After visiting the site we had a kick around with some of the local village kids, some crazy skills they have, and then back to the house for dinner and an early night. The house was so simple, no running water or electricity and a simple squatting out house at the back. It was very different, I don't think I could live like that but quite a learning experience. The host family were a husband and wife with 3 children, a daughter who I'd guess was about 10 who helped with the cooking and washing, a son about 4 and a baby girl as well. They were all very welcoming, although they didn't really speak English we got along well with plenty of smiling and laughter.

PD 2 - We started really early to avoid the sun and basically spent all day shifting rocks......big rocks. In the sun the work was exhausting but it really felt worthwhile. I was shifting with Willhard, the project organiser, and 2 other volunteers, Craig and Neil. By the time of our first break we had moved a lot of the rocks. I couldn't help thinking the in the UK this part of the job would be completed in about 30 mins with one man and a JCB. After our breakfast break Neil managed to squash one of his hands under a rock but still managed to help out one-handed, a really good effort.

By the end of the day we were all knackered. The original plan was for the other volunteers to come and meet us in the village to go and play football with the local school afterwards but sadly the others couldn't come and meet us so the game was called off, shame really as I was looking forward to it. The trip back to Iringa was in a horrible Land-Rover with no suspension and on really bad roads. It was better that the bus but I wouldn't really call it comfortable. Back at the house the girls were having a "girls' night in" so I crashed it and became an honorary sister for the night. Pretty much just chilled out, couple of beers, crap music and an early night. There are two volunteer houses; the one I am in is the townhouse, so called as it is right in the middle of Iringa town centre which is great. The other one is based just on the edge of town, it's about a 20min bus ride and then another 15 minute walk after that. The upside of that house is that there is slightly more space, it's cleaner and you are guaranteed a hot shower. In the townhouse we have a 50-50 chance of there being water, when there is water there is about a 50-50 chance of that water being hot, when it is hot it is almost always scalding so you end up having one of those showers where you are just jumping in and out, burning or freezing yourself! When I arrived back I set about fixing the house, I took the sink apart and unblocked it, swept the floor, cleaned the kitchen and made an ashtray out of tin foil. After that we set some new rules including no cigarette butts in the sink (reason it was blocked) and general tidiness. I became the man of the house!

PD 3 - In the morning we went to the Star school - it is a private school that I was later to learn we were meant to be teaching in. Due to it being a private school a lot of the volunteers didn't really want to teach there. When I went for a look I was amazed. It is shocking how little even the best schools have, no equipment, just a chalkboard and a teacher. They were still sharing something as basic as a ruler, it was really bad. I think it is just as important to help these kids as well as the orphans. These kids are the ones that stand a chance to make a difference in the future so by helping out we are giving them the best chance possible. All morning and all day I was feeling pretty rough. I think all of the travelling and the stuff I have seen over the last week finally caught up with me. I went to Neema for some lunch and Skyped with Kinga which was really good. I was feeling very emotional and I found myself crying a little when telling her about how bad things are over here but I think I needed the release. It's amazing how all these things build up inside of you, tired and run down all it took was a little bit of home to bring it all out. In the evening there was another leaving party at Shooters, I was feeling pretty beat up after the day's work so I just popped in for the longest beer I ever had. The food took about two hours to come so by then I wasn't even hungry. I left and went to bed hoping I'd feel good in the morning. It seems 2 hours is the standard for food delivery so if you decide to eat out then make sure you have plenty of time. I have probably said it before and am sure I will say it again, time is something you have plenty of in Africa!

PD 4 - In the morning we visited the local AIDS Clinic, pretty inspiring stuff. We were lucky to meet the lady who started the whole project, Sister Michaela from Italy. We were showed around and explained every step of the way about what happens there. From testing, counselling, treatment and education it all happens there. They gave us a leaflet with information on how it is doing and it shows in the last few years the percentage of people who have tested positive has dropped from 50% to around 30% which is still very high but it does show that education is working. They said the hardest part is persuading people to get tested, especially from the villages, but I guess a lot of people would rather live in ignorance. We went for lunch at Neema's, as usual it took forever and then in the afternoon we visited the orphanage in Ipamba. This one is quite far out of town so we had to take a dala dala (mini bus or matutu in Kenya) there. In contrast to the other orphanage this one is impeccably run by the church. We walked in and there were loads of kids wanting to play with us. On the way in I noticed the church out front, I assume for the kids and the organisers, but was also really impressed with the fact they had a small farm there to grow their own fruit and vegetables to feed a lot of them. When we first went in the kids ran straight to us and went crazy as Susy had bought a bag full of toys - the closest thing I can compare it to was the feeding of the crocodiles at the park in Mombasa. They were grabbing and pulling the bag apart, screaming to get in to the toys. I was really surprised as I had been told they were really good kids but they had suddenly turned feral! What followed was even more amazing as after all the fighting and the toys had all gone we walked into the nursery where all the babies were sleeping and most of the toys that they had fought for had just been placed in there for the babies. I didn't really understand what the massive melee was about but they were taking them to give to the other kids that were sleeping. That to me was pretty amazing. We popped our heads into a couple of nurseries to see some sleeping babies then came back out to play with the older ones a bit more - they were amazed by my watch and my sunglasses. It was great fun watching them play around with the glasses and I think I got some good pics but it was hard to see how we could help because apart from amusing the kids for a few hours we weren't really doing anything. We left to get a dala dala back to town and waited for a loooooooong time, about one hour but in the direct sunlight it felt like three. When one finally turned up we were relieved and got on. About two hours later it finally started moving and taking us home. Little buses over here are very different, they turn up at any time and leave when they are full so the trip home took about three hours, crazy! Can't remember what we did in the evening but probably involved going to Shooters!

PD 5 - I had a free morning so spent it wandering around Iringa and checking out the local stalls. There is a food market selling fruit, vegetables and dried fish, the smell is atrocious but enjoyable. In the afternoon we went to back to the Upendo orphanage to play with the kids, I took a football along so we could have a kick around. It was great to see Ali again, full of life as always. One of the volunteers had taken a pack of balloons along which they loved, great to play with and so easy to pack. After leaving the orphanage we climbed up to a place called Gangilonga rock (translates to the whispering rock) which is a big rock to sit and watch the sunset. It was quite an easy climb and quite fun. The sunset was slightly disappointing but enjoyed it all the same.

PD 6 - FISCH Saturday Club. FISCH - Future for Iringa street children is an amazing project. It helps kids who find themselves on the streets to educate themselves and tries to re-home them. As well as accepting kids who find them. A lot of time is spent going out and finding street kids who don't know what or where FISCH is. The Saturday club is a chance for any street children to turn up, play some games, have a bible study and then they get some food. I found it very hard to work here, a lot of the kids seem to just turn up for the meal and are not interested in the rest. It was very hard as they don't really speak any English so I couldn't communicate and a lot of the time it felt quite awkward. The beginning was quite fun as there was some younger ones there and we played some football but the afternoon was really hard. I found it really hard to communicate with the kids and I felt a fair amount of hostility towards us. For lunch we went back to the project home and served their food which was pretty enjoyable. The rest of the day was pretty lazy as not much happens on the week-end and the other girls were away on safari so I had a cheap meal with Rachel at the hotel and went to bed.

PD 7 - Sunday, not much happens on a Sunday so I went on a trip to see a Stone Age site. Some crazy rock pillars, old tools, a walk through a river bed and a few crazy looking lizards. I had my first bora bora ride which is as many people as possible on a motorbike. At first it was quite scary but I settled into it. We took a short cut though someone's front garden which was quite fun but otherwise a pretty uninteresting day. As much as it was good to have seen the rocks and the old stone age tools it was all a little boring. A small note on the day happened on the dala dala home. Sat at the bus stop were two plastic buckets each with a bloody cow's head in. Hidaya explained to me that they use them for stock and I didn't think of it again until I sat at the back of the bus. I heard the guys loading the back and then felt something on the back of my head. Turning sharply I was suddenly face to horn with a dead cow. They packed both heads right behind me and we were on our way. I did not really enjoy that ride being attacked by flies and having that under me, but this is Africa and stuff like this is normal!

PD 8 - We woke up in the morning and were just chatting when Rachel mentioned Halloween, instantly we all seemed to have the same idea and the Halloween party was on. I love carving pumpkins and came up with the idea of carving watermelons instead. Then Rachel said we should all dress up and it suddenly sounded like the best party ever! We had some Plasticine in the house so we made some little Halloween decorations and just chatted about various ideas. In the afternoon I went with Susy, Lucy and Ebru out to the construction project in the village again. We managed to lay a few more rocks and spent the night with the family there. I think the construction project has been my favourite so far as I really feel I am doing something there as opposed to just visiting the kids.

PD 9 - Waking up early we went to the project and lumped a few more rocks around. The main foundations on the accommodation block had been finished so we started on the outer wall for the main classroom. It was great to see they had had some professional builders in and had been working on the chicken hatchery which is coming along really well. We had lunch then back to town. Luckily this time we had a proper taxi rather than the crappy Land-Rover with no suspension so whilst I still wouldn't have called it comfort, it was much nicer. In the evening we went to the hotel for a meal and upon our return our next new arrivals had arrived in the house, Jamie and Holly. Also two others who used to stay with us had returned for a couple of nights as they didn't like Dar Es Salaam. We went to Shooters that night for a few drinks as a welcome and a welcome back kind of thing and played a few games of pool.

PD 10 - I have to be honest and say that no volunteering took part this day, it was all about Halloween partying. In the morning we went out to buy some watermelons to carve, a couple of pineapples and some snacks for all the people coming. We emptied out the watermelons and made a punch with it by mashing it up, adding vodka, Sprite and a little bit of fresh pineapple and I have to say it was pretty damn amazing. I carved two watermelons and a pineapple. The chunks of pineapple I cut out I put on cocktails sticks and stabbed them into it, kind of like a Halloween hedgehog thing, massively retro! After all that was prepared we set about our costumes, it was essential to dress up, except for Willard and Ino (locals who look after the volunteers) as they had never heard of Halloween. Originally I was going to dress up as a ghost but as we were walking around I saw some plastic piping and thought it'd be a good idea to tie that around me as a support, drape orange fabric over me and be a pumpkin. With a little help I got it into shape and my costume was made, looked crappy, but a crappy pumpkin! Rachel gave me some brown leggings and I bought a green basket to go on my head and I was good to go. Rachel made a really good corpse bride outfit, Holly was a spider, Lucy a witch, we had zombies, a cat, a mummy and a couple of ghosts - it was a fantastic effort all round. The night kicked off at 7:30, I had rigged a little thing at the door to fall on people so they'd scream, worked a treat. The party went really well, our African friends were very confused when they walked in, it's amazing what you can achieve on such a small budget. When all the booze had finished we went over to Shooters for a couple and then I was bundled into a taxi to go the Twisters (local nightclub). I had said I wasn't going and I was hoping not to go there at all during my time in Iringa but I didn't have much choice. Expecting the worst we arrived and went to but I was pleasantly surprised. As you walk in there is a large outside bar area witch is very chilled and the dancing area is a room off to the left. After getting a drink I was told we were dancing so in we went. I won't go into all the details but I had a dance off and then a dance circle going, my moves were pretty damn awesome and we all had an amazing time. When the time to go home came I hopped on a bora bora, back of a motorcycle, with Holly and we were driven home. I know it doesn't sound safe but it was an awesome ride, I love bora boras! All in all it was a fantastic day.

PD 11 - At some point during the previous night I had agreed to go out to the construction project in the morning. Stupid idea as the car picked us up at 9am and it was packed with nine of us in there. Having been to the village a couple of times I also knew that it was an awful, bumpy ride. Still, I manned up and off we went. Today we were digging the trenches for more foundations which involved plenty of hoeing and of course many jokes about hoes. On the way home we stopped off and had a football game against the local school which was really good - I brought my A game and scored our only goal with a cheeky back heel, it ended 1-1. We had the school's head teacher on our side, I think he loved the opportunity to kick the kids because he held nothing back. I managed to put my hangover aside for the time we were playing football but the minute we stopped I felt worse than ever so the car journey back was hell, I just about held it together. A quiet night was appreciated and we all got an early bed.

PD 12 - Friday morning, there were lots of plans to do stuff with various groups but they all seemed to fall through. We had breakfast at the hotel, best one ever, they actually had everything and then I went shopping as it was my last chance to get souvenirs. We had lunch at Neema's paired with a massive rain storm and another night out. I think by this point I was struggling with the volunteering - there are many reasons for this but basically more structure is needed. I wish I'd had more time in Iringa to pick a project and really get stuck into it but I didn't give myself enough time, more advice before I left about what to expect would have helped. I managed to buy some amazing fabric from a local store and had a local seamstress make me some pants and pyjama bottoms. It's amazing how many seamstresses there are here, they're on every corner. The fabric I bought is bright green with leaves and birds on it so they are proper Afro jungle-pants.

PD 13 - With no volunteering to be done, we headed out to Udzungwa for two nights to visit some amazing waterfalls. The trip out there took a hell of a long time, luckily I was late home so I could sleep on the bus. A couple of standout moments on the journey were when a guy put his foot in Jamie's face and when Jamie then got assaulted by a coconut man!! Because they store a lot of luggage on top of the bus the guys working have to climb up and down, usually they have a ladder, but this time they didn't. To get up and down they would stand on the window frames, apart from when they miss and the skanky, unclothed foot flies through the window and scrapes its ugly toenails right down Jamie's cheek. Amusingly he has a foot phobia and was quite close to throwing up, I found it very entertaining!! The other incident was on the dala dala. Jamie being a proper mzungu was riding with his head out the window when from nowhere a guy chased him down looking very threatening with a coconut like he was about to smash it over his head! Once again I, and the rest of the bus, found this very funny. Luckily he couldn't catch the bus up so nothing happened. Ironically he had said to me about 10 seconds earlier that he thought someone was about to chop his head off with a machete, I think he must have meant coconut. After about eight hours travelling we finally arrived where we would be staying, Hondo Hondo, and it was beautiful. Thatched huts, in the middle of nowhere, very peaceful. We had a full three course meal and then they bought the breakfast menu to pre-order from. Oh my god this menu was awesome, finally a proper breakfast, black pudding and everything. After dinner we went to bed ready for an early start but I couldn't sleep, it felt like the night before Christmas and my gift is a full breakfast!!

PD 14 - The day started about 7am with a breakfast of kings before we went hiking. We set off to the national park base and signed up to a 7km hike. None of us were too sure what to expect but we were all amazed by the end of the day. It was so hot and hard going to begin with but we were seeing some cool stuff to keep us motivated. We saw giant red legged millipedes, giant African snails (and I mean giant), monkeys and all sorts. After about three hours we finally reached the first waterfall - they take you to the furthest away first which is a good idea. The fall was not overly impressive to look at but the good point is but we could swim so we all dived in and played around. The water was so cold but definitely refreshing after such a hike! A few pics later we were on our way to our second water fall, it was breathtaking. They took us to the top of the waterfall and due to the lack of water at this time of year we could just walk all over the rocks. We were on the top plateau and the view was astounding. However, just below us was a second shelf and from there you could look all the way down so I decided that was where I wanted to go. I backtracked and found a route across the river and then a small track down and there I was, staring down from about 150m up off the edge of a waterfall.....I was scared. I often get the heebie-jeebies when at the edge of large heights, people often ask if I have a fear of heights. I don't think I do, I think I have a fear of falling from heights! For some reason to really scare myself up I always seem to imagine myself doing handstands on the edge of stupidly high things which really doesn't help. Holly and Jamie worked their way down to join me on the bottom part but on the way Holly somehow managed to get her hair caught in some twigs. It was quite impressive, they were like thorns and Holly has a lot of hair so it took a long time to unwind her. After chilling out at the top and eating my sandwich, made from breakfast leftovers, we were off again. The next stop was from the bottom looking up and then another viewpoint on the way back, all in all a pretty stunning hike. Upon our return we had another three course meal (I love it when it's all-inclusive) and ordered another amazing breakfast and planned the following day. Rather than getting the bus back we all chipped in to get a taxi, this meant that we had time in the morning for another trek, this time looking for monkeys. We were taken into the forest, and I mean forest. This time there were no trails, no paths and we had to hack through stuff to get to where we were going. I loved it, it felt like being a proper explorer. Our guide took us over rocks, up steep inclines, piles of poo, apparently elephant poos. I find it really hard to believe that elephants can live in mountainside forests but I have seen the evidence and I now believe, crazy! Anyway, we found the monkeys and spent an hour watching them play, sleep, groom, masturbate in their natural habitat, it was great to see and I felt like a wildlife presenter. After an hour or so in their company it was time to go back and get the taxi to Iringa. The taxi ride was quite frustratingly slow but we made it and it was a lot easier than catching buses. The evening was my last night in Iringa so we all went out for dinner to Sai Villa again, had a lovely meal and then just home to bed. I did get to try Tanzanian wine, called Dodoma, which was a lot better than I expected.

PD 15 - Lucy, Jamie and Adele walked me to the station in the morning, I was really sad to go, I had such a great time in Iringa, but it's time to move on with the trip. I am slightly nervous as I created a nice little comfort zone and now it is time to leave it behind. It has been great to meet the people and get used to being Africa, I feel a lot more confident than I did in Kenya so its nervous excitement I'd guess you could say. On to the unknown.......

Side note - I can't remember what day it was but I went to Shooters to watch Man U. vs. Chelsea, so much fun. It seems everyone in Africa is a fan of one of those teams, the atmosphere was electric. What was great fun was that every time a goal went in the bar-man played some music and all the fans were dancing - if you did that in England you'd be attacked! Shame the match was marred by some really bad refereeing.

Just in case you should ever find yourself in Iringa I have listed a few places to eat.

Shooters
Oh the home from home, a crazy bar/restaurant where we'd often eat and jump onto the "Konyagi Train". Most nights out started here, many ended here! A few good characters around, Frank who worked there was always a

top guy and it was pretty cheap. Great place to go and play pool or watch the football. On the downside, food on average took about 1 1/2 hours, apart from one time when the food didn't even come! Still, this is Africa. Not a great place but many happy memories.

Sai Villa
Ate here twice, this is the "posh" restaurant, amusingly has Kentucky Fried Chicken on the menu. Had two nice meals and managed to get a bottle of Dodoma, a Tanzanian red wine, pretty average, fruity with a dry finish. Had my leaving meal here and it had fantastic jungle toilets.

The Hotel
We had breakfast here a lot as it was only 3000 shillings (£1) for eggs, toast, fruit, juice and coffee. Sadly most of the time they didn't have most of the stuff. I didn't really understand why we kept going back there but I just went with the flow. We had dinner a few times, I always ordered the pepper steak but they never had it. Apparently it was great but I'll never know. A good option for a cheap feed.

Mama's Kitchen
A real locals place in the market, you have to be shown where it is. It's not actually called Mama's Kitchen but our group had adopted one of the cooks and called her Mama. I am not actually sure what it is called. I went there for breakfast once to eat chapatis, like mini naan breads but with sugar which were nice. The other time we went as a group and it was hard work. I am starting to think I don't really like proper African cuisine, but I'll keep trying. This place was a house favourite, not really mine, but a must visit if you want an authentic, African meal and experience.

Hondo Hondo
Now we're talking. All the food here was included in the package. Dinner first night, soup, stroganoff and flambéed bananas, all lovely. Second night pancakes with ratatouille, pork chops with amazing seasoning and banana cake for dessert. Breakfast was another level, maybe because I have been missing it but bacon, sausage, beans, black pudding, FRIED BREAD, fresh pressed watermelon juice, perfect. Also all served whilst watching wild baboons playing and eating about 15 metres away from you. An amazing experience, if you are passing through Tanzania take the time to find this place on the outskirts of the Udzungwa National Park where you can do the monkey trekking and waterfalls.

10. Day 23 - Mbeya

Day 23 - On to Mbeya

A quick note of interest, it seems around here that it is perfectly normal for two men to hold hands. I have seen it quite a lot and it simply means they are good friends. However you never see a man and a woman holding hands, just an interesting culture difference. Anyway, originally I had planned to go to Zanzibar for a few days and get the train from Dar Es Salaam today, however I was having such a good time in Iringa that I decided to stay there and catch the train in Mbeya instead. I am really happy that I did as my last few days have been amazing.

Looking back on my time in Iringa makes me so sad that I have had to move on, from the moment I arrived the people there made me feel so welcome and over the last few weeks I have met some people who I hope will be in the rest of my life. I put it down to the fact that it takes a certain type of person to want to volunteer, they're my type of people. This added to the fact that they are doing it in Africa means that they are an adventurous type so before I met them we had some things in common. Some of the volunteers were so pro-active and out doing stuff everyday but others basically did nothing, just hung around and had a good time - I'd put myself somewhere in the middle. I feel that I could have done more but I don't think I gave myself enough time to really get stuck into any of the projects. There were so many options it took a week or more to see them all before you can even decide what to get involved in. The projects need a bit more structure and information for people before you arrive to help you, and the kids, get the most out of your time there. The great thing is as a group we all agreed this and there are movements underway to get some structure going so I feel really good to have been a part of it. If you are reading this because you are thinking of volunteering in Africa then stop thinking and just DO IT. The people you help, the people you meet helping will simply change your life, the fact that you are thinking of it already means you should be there.

Anyway, the bus journey to Mbeya was your standard, uncomfortable seats, sat next to a fat man only this time we also broke down for two hours which wasn't fun. I am surprised I haven't broken down until now as I was expecting it to happen regularly. I found myself hanging around by the side of the road in the blistering heat with no shade. My only form of entertainment was a crazy lady running around trying to sell me mangoes, it was an experience, not one I'd want to repeat. I was a little concerned before I came out here about breakdowns and how to deal with them. Honestly, it is nothing to worry about, it happened, it will probably happen again, but you just get on with it. We arrived in Mbeya at about 5pm and I grabbed a tuk tuk to the GR City hotel. The tuk tuk driver tried to charge me 10,000 shillings so I laughed at him and said I'd pay 5,000, still too much but he didn't argue. It was my fault really as I forgot to agree a price before getting on the tuk tuk. The hotel I really liked, nothing special but for the first time I have met really cheerful staff. I checked into my room then went to dinner in the hotel restaurant. Had a lovely beef salad followed by pepper steak, a very well cooked meal. After dinner I had my first taste of Indian whisky at the bar, I like to try different things when given the chance, I was quite impressed! After dinner I went back upstairs and just passed out, it's mad how I had slept all day but was still tired. It was nice to have a TV again, I got to see all the weekend's Premier League highlights and then fell asleep watching coverage of Obama winning the US election.

African Toilets
There are a few variations, you get your regular western style and your squat and plops but what gets me is the incredible lack of toilet paper which combined with a regular lack of running water causes a problem (a problem that luckily I have yet to be caught out on). It would seem that in your dodge pot squat and plop there's always a bucket with some water but no toilet paper or running water. I can only assume that you are meant to dip your hand in the bucket and give your bum a clean. But then what? Back in the bucket? How many people have used that bucket? Are you meant to double dip? I don't quite get it. The civilised squatter ploppers have toilet paper which is fine. Luckily my Mum advised me to take toilet paper so I have been ok. Luckily I held it all in on the train otherwise that could have given me an experience that would have been quite a large entry for the diary!

Things learnt on Day 23;
1) Transport does break down.
2) Don't worry when it does, just enjoy the chance to stretch your legs.
3) Have a good book on you at all times for when it does.
4) Remember to get a price from the tuk tuk driver before entering the tuk tuk.
5) If you are staying in Mbeya I can recommend staying and eating at the GR City hotel.

11. Day 24 - Train through Zambia

Day 24 - Train to Zambia

I woke up quite early and watch all the election stuff, well done Barak, before going down for breakfast. Saw the same lovely staff, especially one guy in housekeeping, he was very smiley and talkative. I was able to say hi, how are you in Swahili and he loved it, he asked me if I spoke Swahili to which I was honest and said no. I explained that I only knew a few words like "hello" and "where are the toilets" but he spoke to me in Swahili anyway! There was a fair amount of laughing so I have no idea what he was saying but a lot of fun. After breakfast had my first proper hot shower in weeks which was amazing, then went for a walk. I found a place with internet access, which was good as I knew I was going to Lusaka but had nowhere to stay or knew anything about Lusaka. I was at least able to book myself a hostel. Once this was done it was off to the train station to get my 1pm train. Being a good English travelling boy I arrived in plenty of time to ensure I could get my ticket, about 12:30pm. It was good that I got there in plenty of time as when I picked the ticket up I was informed the train wouldn't be arriving until 5pm. Great, four hours to kill but at least not unexpected as I have read a lot about this train being delayed. The station was quite large, just one simple hall with a few benches in with people asleep on them. At the far end of the hall was a television showing some kind of Nigerian soap opera. The toilets were at the opposite end and smelt so bad you couldn't lose them, I am not sure if they have ever been cleaned.

The upside of this massive delay is that it gave me plenty of time to revise. As I mentioned earlier I am doing this trip as part of a career change. I have worked in the hospitality industry for years in various positions and various places around the UK and America. It has given me the chance to meet some great people and see some amazing places. Unfortunately, the main point of working in hospitality is serving people, now I don't know if it is the recession or society but basically people don't seem to be nice any more so it's time for a change. I am revising for an advanced level wine qualification which is the book that I have bought with me, the only book I have bought with me. So far this book has got me through hangovers, bus trip and breakdowns and now a train delay, sadly, because it is a text book, it turns out it is much more boring than watching a Nigerian soap opera when you don't understand the language. The hope is by then end of this trip I will have read the book and pass the exam I have booked one week after I return and embark on my new career in the wine industry. That will be after my second trip which will be around Asia.

5pm came and went, then at 6pm a train pulled up and everyone rushed to get on, at last. Sadly this wasn't my train, it was the train going the other way! Finally at 7pm my train turned up so I rushed to get on. Being the only person in the station this wasn't too hard. As it turns out being on the train isn't too different to being in the station, it just sat there, motionless. Another hour passed, and another before finally someone kind of official looking told me it will be leaving but it will only be a couple more hours. I am sitting here writing this and it's currently 12:22am and we have only just pulled away about 10 minutes ago. Sadly we have stopped again so I have no idea how long this journey is going to take. We are currently running about 11hrs late, I hope we don't get in to the station at midnight, being in a strange town, alone, everything shut, I don't like the sound of that. Lucky I booked that room in Lusaka as I don't think I'll arrive in time to check in! In Iringa Abbas helped me book the ticket over the phone, he speaks fluent Swahili as he was born in Dar. I booked a first class ticket but when I went to pick the ticket up they couldn't get me one so I am in 2nd class, sharing my cabin with a guy called Robin. The cabin should sleep six people, really small space for each person but luckily there is just the two of us in here. Anyway, train is underway again, I am lying on a very uncomfortable bench with no sleeping bag or pillow, at least they give us a blanket each...just in case it gets cold? I am sweating here! Oh well the time has come to try and get some sleep - I am travelling at last! Goodnight.

Things learnt on day 24

1) Learn a few words of the local language so you can initiate some interactions.

2) Appreciate a hot shower when you get the chance to have one.

3) Don't expect the trains to be on time......ever.

4) Don't expect the train to move once you have boarded it.

5) If you book a first class ticket don't bank on getting it.

6) Try not to lose your sleeping bag in Dar, you'll appreciate it on the train.

12. Day 25 - Still on the Train

Day 25 - No idea where but think in Zambia

It's 5am and we have just been woken up by the passport people, first of all you need to be signed out of Tanzania, which was fine, you are then meant to get you new visa for Zambia. They come onto the train in 2 groups, Tanzanian exit people first followed by the Zambian entry people. Sadly the Zambian visa lady breezed past our cabin before we even realised. Luckily I had a little panic attack and realising what might happen if the visas got screwed up I chased them down to give them $50 for a visa. Had I not done so and missed the entrance stamp I would have been in a massive pickle, illegal entry is not something they look upon kindly around here!! But all is well and with another new stamp in my passport, I am going to try to get some more zzzzzz's.

Day 25 – a little later and more awake

So it's now 11ish, train still going, still got a long way to go. The guy I am sharing with, Robin, has had some visa problems. He is dual nationality, South African and British. As it turns out South Africans don't have to pay for a visa into Zambia but British do, the snag is that the Zambian visa lady said that Zambia as a country doesn't recognise dual nationality. Because Robin entered Tanzania on his British passport the exit stamp from Tanzania is also on his British passport. Now the lady on the Zambian side has said that because the exit stamp from Tanzania is on the British passport, he now has to enter Zambia as British meaning he has to pay the $50. Understandably he refused and a big argument broke out and ended up in him nearly getting kicked off the train. The immigration people grabbed his bag and were literally removing him but he was refusing to budge and in the end the immigration people left and the train got going again. We are still not sure if they had the legal power to remove him from the train or if they were trying to intimidate him into giving them $50. The real kicker is that his previous visit to Zambia was on his SA passport, so if they don't recognise dual nationality and they have already stamped his SA passport once before surely that should be the only one that exists and his entry should be free. Robin is now understandably worried about what's going to happen when we get off as they check passports. Neither of us really know what is going to happen but I guess we'll find out in a few, well probably 10, hours! The cabin has been better than expected, Robin knows the manager of the train from his previous journey and has managed to get upgraded from third class to second and into my cabin. We are meant to be sharing with 4 other people but somehow he has managed to persuade the carriage man (all carriages have one staff member looking after them but I am not sure what they are called) to let no-one else in our cabin. I am guessing that he paid him off but I don't know how much it cost so it is just the 2 of us with plenty of space. That has made the journey so far much easier.

Things learnt on day 25

1) Remember to work out how much you need to spend on visa's and keep the money in dollars as it is the only payment they will accept, keep cash with you at all times!
2) Nothing else.

13. Day 26 - Livingstone I presume

Day 26 - Jollyboys

Well I am finally in Livingstone!! After 48hrs of travelling by train, dala dala and bus I have finally arrived. So the last time I had written we were just crossing the border. Robin is still.with me, we travelled all the way here together but he has still to get his visa stuff sorted so for now that is a side story. The train ride itself was looooong, but good. It was quite an up and down experience, you'd have moments when you wanted the train to crash just for a bit of entertainment but other times were optimistic and enjoyable. Would've been a little more so if they had cold beer - just to tease us they had beer but it was all hot as the fridges didn't work. They had filled them with ice but by the time I got onto the train it had unsurprisingly all melted. It's funny over here, when I was ordering beers in the bar in Iringa they would always ask if I wanted it cold or from the shelf, room temperature. I can only assume due to lack of electricity, a lot of people don't have refrigerators so they get used to, and enjoy warm beer. Breakfast was ok, sausage, egg, bread and coffee, but was slightly awkward as we had pulled into a station and had a group of about six kids begging us for money or food through the window while we eat our breakfast. It's a really hard one as I don't want to just give away money to them as it simply encourages them to beg more, but you see others on the train doing it all the time and it's probably a major source of their family's income. Also when people do give it out it is often to a group which then just encourages them to fight as there isn't enough for everyone. I have seen that quite a lot and helped me decide that I wouldn't throw things to the kids off the train. I did feel pretty bad sat right in front of them, eating. Luckily (for us) the train pulled away after just a little while.

The rest of the day was spent reading, moving from carriage to carriage, napping, drinking warm beer and watching an awful Thai kung-fu movie in the bar carriage. The food generally has been pretty awful but a highlight was when we asked if we could just get a bowl of chips and they freshly made fried chicken and chips for us, makes me think it is always worth asking. Otherwise it has been pretty damn boring. The train finally arrived into New Kapiri Mposhi at 1:30am so that totalled nine hours waiting for the train and then 28 hours on the train. I am glad I changed my plans as if I went with the original idea of catching it from Dar Es Salaam, I would have probably slit my wrists by the end of it! New Kapiri Mposhi is a small town built around the end of the train line, it is about a 3hr drive away from Lusaka (capital of Zambia). I have no idea why they stop the train here which seems in the middle of nowhere rather than run it a little longer into Lusaka but that's the way it is. One of my concerns has been how to get from NKM to Lusaka as I haven't been able to find any information about it. The later the train was getting the more worried I was getting, where in the world do you get buses at 1:30am in the morning? At worst I guessed I'd be sleeping in the train station for the night. Probably would be just as comfortable as the train. However, this is Africa and they know what you need.

At 1:30am there was a bus waiting to go to Lusaka where we needed to get to so we could transfer to Livingstone. Well I say bus, I mean fully packed dala dala with Robin and me riding shotgun with my 80litre backpack on our laps - this thing was chocka. We were promised it would only take two hours so as expected it took about three and a half hours. The dala dala dropped us off right at the bus station we needed to be at for further travel onto Livingstone which was great. We arrived about 5:30am and the next bus was at 6:30am, the only problem is that we had no cash. There were various people around that were more than happy to exchange some dollars for me if I needed but Robin didn't have any and needed a cash machine, given the exchange rates I thought this would be the best thing for me to do as well. Slightly up against it time-wise we asked around and got pointed in the right direction by a taxi driver. Running down to the machine I managed to get some money out but Robin couldn't, turns out that no cash point we found would accept MasterCard. We rushed back to the bus station, bought our tickets and managed to get on a bus to Livingstone. The bus station, although nowhere near as bad as Dar, is also quite an intimidating place. There are lot of different companies running the same route with various styles and quality of busses. We asked our dala dala driver which one he would recommend and he dropped us off right at their ticket shack. All the companies seem to be about the same price so if you can't get any recommendation then just look around for a nice looking bus then track down their ticket shack, just have some cash with you and leave plenty of time. Quite surprisingly the bus left bang on time and another six and a half hours later, bang on 48 hours after I arrived at the train station, I had made it to Livingstone. To be fair, given the regularity of breakdowns and delays I am quite pleased with that.

Once we were dropped off we wandered over and I checked into the hostel I will be staying for the next five days, it was easy to find from the bus drop off. Love it so far. A lot of people I have met along the way recommended this place and I was looking at it before I came out here. There is a nice swimming pool, bar, restaurant, garden with mango trees, I don't think I will have to leave this place, I'll be happy chilling by the pool, reading my book, supping on a cold one for a few days. Hopefully there will be some cool people as well. Just as I have written that a group of about eight Japanese have turned up who were on the same train as me from Mbeya, looks like a family holiday. I am planning to sit around the bar, meet people and see how that goes. Right now I am not feeling too sociable though.

After a quick dip in the pool and a beer I went for a walk to get some cash and check out the local area. Same as the rest of the Africa I have seen (except Iringa) you seem to get harassed all the way by people trying to sell you stuff. Something I won't miss when I get home is people saying "hey brother" "hey my friend", "let me help you", I am getting better at telling them where to go though, it's harmless but gets annoying. I find some days I will be really patient and handle them with ease but other days I get angry with them. It's a pain as I know they are only trying to make a living.
I guess that's it for now, I expect a few boring days before the safari!

Things learnt on day 26
1) You have to make your own choice about whether you take things to throw out to kids from the train, but make sure you take plenty or expect some fights!
2) The beer on the train is warm.
3) You may be able to negotiate with the cabin staff for some privacy.
4) Thai kung fu movies are entertainingly bad.
5) Take plenty of snacks.
6) And toilet paper.

7)	Onward travel is often easier than you'd expect and at worst you sleep a few hours in a train station.

8)	MasterCard doesn't seem to be accepted in many cash machines in Zambia, make sure you have a Visa or plenty of cash just in case.

14. Day 30 - What to do in Livingstone

Day 30 - So much for boring!

I was worried that my time would be boring here but so far I am having a blast, hence the complete lack of writing in here for quite some time! It's not been go go go, there has been my fair share of just sitting around doing nothing and studying but time here flies. So, what's been going on?

My first day here was just strolling around. I visited the craft market which is constant harassment to buy from their stand - you hear many stories of how poor they are and how they need you to buy something so they can afford the bus home. Just be ready for it as it will make you feel bad and I ended up buying some African art. It is funny how they say they have made them themselves yet they all look the same on other stalls just with a different name carved on the bottom. It's almost like they get the same stock and just carve their own name on it, but they wouldn't do that, would they? After I caved in and bought my giraffe I continued to walk, only now I had a bag so the others knew I have spent money and may spend more so the harassment stepped up a notch. If you can deal with it and are in a patient mood the craft market is worth a visit, if you are having a bad day I'd stay away. While walking along in Livingstone it seems to depend what side of the road you are on as to whether or not you get hassled. After a few trips I have now managed to plot a hassle free-ish route to the main centre from the hostel, although there are always a couple of guys stood right outside the hostel.

Robin went to get his immigration issues sorted, apart from a small scare when one of the officers shouted "throw him in jail". We think when they said that they were testing the waters to see if they could get a bribe out of him but he got away with it and was given a two day visa at no cost. Lucky! In the evening we went to a local family's house for dinner. It was someone that Robin had met on a previous train journey, he seems to know a lot of people. We were picked up by a taxi, driven into deepest Livingstone and welcomed into their house. The husband, Abdi, sat and chatted to us whilst dinner was being prepared. They had a cute, but slightly violent, three year-old daughter who I was playing with and about 150 little chickens! He breeds them as a side business to his own import export company. Although the house while we were there had no electricity you could tell they were doing well for themselves. The electric goes off twice a week for a few hours, I think they called it load shedding, but I didn't really understand why, will investigate. The house itself was properly made with real bricks and a proper roof and on the inside there was a 42" TV, PC and Mac, all the stuff you associate with my world. Oh, and they had a maid, a male maid, is that still a maid or a helper? I don't know. Anyway, after an hour or so of chat dinner was served, a lovely beef stew with mashed potatoes, can't beat a bit of home-made mash! Due to all the travelling, this was still the same day I arrived in Livingstone so I had been up since 1am - after dinner I was so tired. I felt a bit bad as I sat there, yawning, but I think they understood and sorted us out a taxi home again. What amazed me is that Robin had spent a few hours with this lady on a train, they had never met me, and they were ready to welcome us into their home, feed us and not only that, knowing Robin's problems, give him some money to help him out. All in all a pretty amazing experience, shame I was so tired.

Once back at the hostel I pretty much went straight to bed.

The next day was a trip to Victoria Falls. I attached myself onto an American girl who I found out was also travelling alone so I'd have someone to chat to, I don't think she minded. She was an air hostess back in the States just taking the opportunity to see some stuff. While there we also met two other guys, Iain and Josh who also hung out with us all day. The falls themselves were pretty disappointing as there is not much water in there at the moment. It hasn't occurred to me that the Victoria Falls suffer from seasons. We are here and it is right at the beginning of the rainy season, which is also the end of the dry season so the falls themselves were running a little dry. I guess to see them in their full glory you need to go at the end of the rainy season. We were also hoping to go to Devil's pool while there but you needed to pay a tour guide and we ran out of time. All the bits that we could walk around had pretty much dried up so it was more like the Victoria Cliffs. Using a little imagination I could manage to get a sense of full force which is pretty spectacular. The disappointment of the falls was fortunately offset by the baboons though. They were everywhere, just walking side by side with us. One in particular just sat on his tree, staring at me, I must have been about two metres away taking photos and he seemed to love it - so many poses!

In the evening we all booked onto the sunset river cruise. The sunset was really bad unfortunately, but we did see elephants and hippos and all the drinks were included so I saw plenty of beer too. On the boat were a group of South Africans who were staying to watch the rugby vs. Ireland. As Josh is half Irish we decided to have a little bet. Whichever team concedes the first point had to go and jump in the swimming pool, I was on the Irish side. Turns out it was one of the best ideas I have had, Ireland got the first points and the South African's all got wet. Rather amusingly there was a German couple who sat quite close to the pool, they got pretty wet too! After being told off by the couple, and the management, it was back to the game. Ireland ended up losing but I don't really care about that. After the game we got a ride back, took a bit longer then we'd expected after a delay due to being held up by elephants in the road. That was a first! The taxi driver was a little afraid, he says it's not the one you see that you have to worry about it's the ones you can't see. Apparently it's been known before for elephants to flip taxis and sit on them, crushing the people inside!

As you can imagine Sunday morning started a little slow, out of bed late and then just sat around the pool all morning. In the afternoon we joined the trip arranged by our hostel to a local orphanage for a game of football. After a look around we met the kids and managed to start the game. The kids were quite a range of ages, from five to eighteen. Once again it was amazing to see how they all look after each other like a family. After watching some traditional dancing we managed to get the game going and I managed to score to keep my 100% scoring record intact, three games three goals! It was a lot of fun playing with the kids afterwards. Sunday evening was just hanging around the hostel and an early night.

Monday I was up at 6am as I had booked myself on a lion and cheetah walk. It was phenomenal. We got to play with the lions, stroke them, rub their bellies and manes and the walk with them holding their tails. To be that close to such a beast, even though he was used to people you could see the power and potential. Luckily they must have already eaten or don't like ginger as I made it through ok. After the lions I got to play with three cheetahs, this was my highlight. They purr! With the cheetahs you could be a bit more playful and rub their heads, it was like playing with a cat at home I was scratching behind the ear, he was licking me. One of the other ladies freaked out as she was bitten, it was just a playful bite though, so nothing to worry about, it's just a feline killing machine! After petting and playing we took them for a walk, posed for a few more pictures and then they ran them. It's almost like a greyhound track, chasing a lure on a wire. They are so fast, it was amazing to see, and hear the sound of the feet pounding the ground was breathtaking. Glad I'm not a gazelle or some other silly grass eater, as there would be no getting away from a cheetah at top speed.

I was back at the camp by 11am and spent the afternoon tracking down a Zambia football shirt. After trying lots of shops a few times I finally managed to get a price I was happy with. In the evening we got chatting to a couple of new arrivals, they did part of the same train ride I did and have been travelling together for a while. They met en route and were going the same way so stuck together, I love how that works. One of my biggest concerns before coming to Africa was meeting people, I was told it would be easy but I didn't realise how easy. I think a big mistake I have made so far is early on in my trip I was staying in cheap hotels rather than hostels. Because of this I have felt quite alone in a lot of places. Hostels are places where other travellers are and where you can meet other people to do things with or at least have a beer with. They will have stories and advice for you but staying in hotels you are generally on your own.

We had a few beers with them until the bar here shut, so we went and found another bar and had a few more beers. It was your typical Afro-night club, 70% men, 25% prostitutes and 5% Westerners being hit on by prostitutes! Josh was getting a fair amount of attention. He enjoyed it at first but was understandably getting a bit annoyed by the end. There were a couple of Korean dudes on the table next to us who left the club separately with different women. I wonder where they have woken up and if they still have all their stuff. The older one left first, then about five minutes after the other one left, both times being led away by a man (I assume a pimp) as well as the lady of the night. Luckily I have a gorgeous fiancée at home so it is not something I even have to think about, but I do wonder what has happened to them, did they get what they paid for or a whole lot more? Maybe I'll try and find them today, if they're still alive.

Well I guess that brings my "boring" time up to date. Today I think I will visit the museum, swim a bit, maybe write some postcards, I have written all this so that's one of my planned activities today achieved. Tomorrow it's off to Devils Pool so this may be my last ever entry, I may fall of the edge of Victoria Falls. I hope I don't, would really put a bad stain on the day.

Things learnt so far in Livingstone.

1) Craft market is nice but it seems the biggest craft is creating stories and sales skills.
2) Be prepared to be offered lots of gifts on the street, Livingstone very touristic.
3) Try to get to Victoria Falls when there is lots of water.

4) Germans don't like beings splashed by South Africans.

5) I can highly recommend the walking with lions and cheetahs experience in Livingstone but it is quite expensive.

6) If you want a Zambia football shirt, shop around and negotiate. Ask your local taxi driver where the best place to buy one is, that worked for me.

7) Beware of overly friendly women in bars, they are often prostitutes, not all of them, but most.

8) Stay in hostels if you are travelling alone and afraid of not meeting people. One of the guys I met gave me the advice that if you are alone in a hostel, grab a beer, find the largest group and just ask if they mind if you join them. This way there will be no pressure on you to talk, you can just listen, learn names, see what they are like, join in if you want but above all as it was the largest group the next day most people around the hostel will know your face and say hello to you. Good advice and it works.

15. Day 34 - Botswana

Day 34 - On the road in Botswana

So I am three days into my organised safari with mixed thoughts. The reason I decided to book the safari was to guarantee that I'd get to the flight in time, however, having been travelling through Africa meeting the people I have I now kind of wish I was still travelling that way, by public transport. On the other hand, I am seeing some amazing things doing it this way, everyone seems pretty nice and it is good to not have to worry about anything. Currently we are whizzing through the Kalahari Desert but I will start this update a few days ago to bring it up to date.

After another evening being hit on by prostitutes (I never did see the Koreans again) then it was an early start to get to the Devils pool. To save money we got the local mini bus which is always an adventure, crammed full of people we pulled away. By now I am kind of used to how it all works and got chatting to a dude in a Denver Bronco's shirt. Turns out he runs one of the local stalls selling tourist tat in the Vic Falls. After another incredibly uncomfortable ride we get to the falls. We had a quick look at Bronco's man's stall out of courtesy and then met up with our Devils pool group, there were six of us. The hike over to the falls was pretty epic. There is a local power station which siphons off a lot of the water from the falls but they were cleaning the turbine so there was more water than usual. We had to cross about a 30m section about the width of a balance beam with a couple of inches of water rushing over our ankles and a 100m drop off the falls about 20m behind us. I don't think I have concentrated so hard on anything in my life. About an hour later after rock hopping, wading and jumping all within

a few metres of death we made it to the pool. Some of the
views on the way there were pretty spectacular but nothing
quite like this. The pool is about three metres deep right on
the cusp of the falls, water falling all around us with a 100
metre drop right next to us. One after another we held our
breath and jumped in. The feeling was of complete
exhilaration and fear, to be sat in a pool staring down from
the top of one of the biggest waterfalls in the world was
stunning. We were in the pool for about 10 minutes posing
for pictures and being bitten by fish before it was time to
head back. The water had been re-diverted to the power
station again so most of it was dry and it only took 20
minutes to get back. An amazing trip and would
recommend it to anyone and everyone.

The afternoon was spent relaxing by the pool, online and
saying bye to the friends I had made at the hostel before
calling my friendly taxi driver (Eric) to take me over to meet
up with the tour group. Eric was the taxi man who was
driving after the sunset cruise when we got held up by an
elephant!
I arrived to meet the rest of the group at the campsite but
they were all out on the sunset/booze cruise. I got to know
a few people who were not going to be in my group and had
dinner with them before watching the football. What I
didn't realize is that pretty much all of the people on the
safari have been doing it for a while, all of the trips from the
north meet in Livingstone before splitting up and continuing
to either Jo'berg or Cape Town. Due to the fact that
everyone knew each other it made it a bit harder to join in
as you are kind of viewed as the outsider. Anyway, back to
the football, Zambia (Chipolopolo) vs. South Africa (Bafana
Bafana) for the Nelson Mandela Cup, a friendly game played

every year. Chipolopolo, Zambia's nickname, means Copper Bullets and they are the reigning Africa Cup of Nations champions as I write this. I was sat at the bar in my Zambia jersey, blending in with the locals (sort of). It turned out to be a good game and fortunately Zambia won, it was a lot of fun wandering around in the jersey getting high fives from a lot of the employees!!

I was shown into the tent I would be spending the next week in, smelt so bad, but I managed to get a few hours sleep. The first day driving was pretty quick, we soon crossed the border into Botswana and then to the campsite. In the afternoon we had a cruise down the Chobe River seeing lots of crocodiles, hippos, buffalo.....and ducks! We even got to see a croc eating a little buffalo floating in the water, the smell was awful but something amazing to see. In the evening we were just relaxing around the campsite before an early night. All the guys who were on the different trip to Cape Town were also at the same campsite that night so it was a big group again. A couple of Danish guys who were at the Jollyboys hostel were on that tour. It was quite funny as they were the guys who also wanted to cancel their tour in order to continue travelling alone. They did the same as I did, booked but wished they hadn't.

In the morning we went on a game drive, my first one and it was pretty special. We managed to see four out of the big five which considering there are no rhinos in Chobe, that's as good as you can get. The big five is something people talked a lot about. It comes from the old days of hunting, big five refers to the most dangerous animals to hunt, so they are; lion, leopard, elephant, buffalo and rhino. It is pretty rare to see a leopard, although it was resting a long way away in a tree, we definitely saw one. The rest of the group have done a few game drives but this was everyone's first time seeing a leopard, they are very elusive. Sadly it was too far away to get a decent photo but still pretty epic. We also saw elephants, boring buffalo, sleepy lions, horny tortoises, loud squirrels and my favourite, dung beetles rolling dung. I've seen it so much before on TV but it was fascinating to see it so close. I still think it's pretty stupid, but amazing how good they are at shaping poo into perfect spheres!

After the game drive we headed back to the campsite for breakfast and to say good-bye to the other group before a short drive (300kms!) down to our next campsite, a place called elephant sands, about 50kms north of Nata, Botswana. We arrived and it is one of those few places where everyone's breath is taken. The campsite is just next to a watering hole and there must have been at least 12 elephants in there. We all jumped off the bus to go and check it out and get some pictures. The bar and pool were about 40 metres back from the hole - it was just something special to be so close and just watch these wild elephants. After the initial excitement died down a little we headed back to set up our tents and have some lunch. After we were fed and housed we headed back to the bar and we all sat around in the pool chatting and watching the elephants. It worked really well as we were forming a new group, the others had all left and it was a great setting to be able to do it.

While we were there the elephants got attacked by a pack of wild dogs, apparently they are very rare too. First of all about four dogs just ran at the elephants but they stood their ground. All of a sudden about three more dogs arrived but the elephants chased them off and they retreated. We thought that was it but they came back and there must have been about 25 dogs just charging the watering hole and the elephants all had to retreat and ran away! So now the dogs were hanging out in the water while the elephants were pushed back. Every now and again an elephant would approach the water making noise but normally it would take just one dog to growl and stand its ground and the elephant would back off. If I were the elephant I'd have probably just stepped on it! For about 15 minutes the dogs dominated the pool. Then, the big one, a massive elephant charged the pool followed by a couple more, the dogs stood firm thinking he was faking but no, he kept on going and the dogs scattered. Pretty quickly other elephants joined in and regained control of the hole. The dogs retreated, for a while they looked like they were planning another attack but something happened in the group and they started fighting each other and disappeared over the horizon. The elephants won! It was a lot of fun just sitting there, relaxing in the pool, well the slimy pool, with a cool beer, watching the elephants. All the water in elephant sands was naturally salty. The reason is millions of years ago the whole area was underwater, salt water, and over the years this has dried up leaving behind massive salt deposits. For some reason this makes the swimming pool slimy, the only downside to the place.

A few hours later we had dinner, which apart from being regularly bombarded by suicidal dung beetles was lovely. We found out that that evening there was due to be a meteor shower, the sky was so clear it would be beautiful. We hung around the bar with the elephants until 10:30pm when the shower was meant to start. The elephants were getting so close to us by now checking us out, we must have been within five metres, one got so close I could reach out and touch it but I though it would be a bad idea and managed to resist the temptation. We headed back to the camp to watch the shower, we grabbed our mattresses out of our tents and just laid on them looking up at the stars. I have never seen so many stars in my life. Due to being in the southern hemisphere I didn't really know which was which constellation, but, luckily there's an app for that! I cracked out my iPad with the night sky app and it was wonderful, you just hold it in front of you and it has a full on star chart with planets as well. By far the brightest object in the sky was Jupiter glimmering away. By 11:30 there were still no meteors so people started to get bored and slowly drift away to bed. In the background you could hear the elephants splashing about.

About 12am there was just Sarah and myself waiting for something to happen, just one meteor would have been good, when we heard a different noise kind of a low grumbling growl. We just froze, worried, trying to work out what the noise was as it sounded close. Fortunately we worked it out to be Mal snoring, so that was a relief. About 10 minutes later we heard another noise, similar but close and louder, we both knew right away that was a lion or leopard for sure. We just looked at each other, both said nothing and ran to our tents, it was almost comical as we even bumped into each other whilst scarpering! I put down all my flaps and tucked myself into my tent. Luckily I was in the tent next to the snoring Mal so I was hoping his growl would intimidate the lions, it was pretty loud! I could hear all kinds of rustling around outside the tent but I was so tired that I still managed to drop off. In the morning I couldn't find my flip-flops anywhere, I was thinking, typical, only I could lose my flip flops in a tent, I usually leave them outside so I thought the lion stole them! As I was walking to breakfast I found them, just where I left them, running away from big cat noises! When we set our tents up we were advised where not to put them as the elephants do walk through at night and sure enough there was a buzz around the group in the morning, one guy had an elephant bump into his tent! Quite a few people were talking about hearing a lion or leopard wandering around the camp as well so at least I know it wasn't just my mind playing with me, or worse, the lion!

Today we are on a medium length drive (480kms) to a place called Martins Drift close to the South Africa border to camp. I guess that's brought everything up to date for now, we are about to stop for lunch.

Learnt here;

1) Do the Devils pool trip. Make sure you book it before you go to the Victoria Falls park as it fills up quickly and if you don't get on it and have to book for a different day you will have to pay the park entrance fee twice.

2) You can do a boat ride or a hiking trip to Devils pool. I highly recommend hiking if you are fit enough.

3) Overland tours are a great way to see a lot in a short amount of time in a safe environment however you will miss a lot of experiences you can only get by mixing in with the locals. I was surprised how many people were travelling alone and how young everyone was.

4) Dung beetles are amazing and slightly suicidal...but then if my life revolved around balls of poo I may be too.

5) Elephant sands is a good stop on the way through Botswana, don't expect luxury, but if you are camping through Africa then you wouldn't be anyway.

6) Don't put your tent next to acacia trees. Elephant scratching posts!

16. Day 35 - Final Boarder

Day 35 - On the road again in South Africa

We have just crossed the border out of Botswana into South Africa, it makes me sad as this is the last country I will be visiting so I feel the trip is nearly over. Last night was pretty good, we arrived at the campsite after our drive, made our little tent village then just chilled in the pool. You can really feel the group getting closer each day. The drive flew by as we all started playing cards, so many people were joining in that we had to split up into two groups giving us a winners' table and a losers' side. Fortunately I was lucky enough to spend most of the game on the winners' table. For dinner we had amazing steak and roast potatoes cooked by our guide and his cooking team. On the bus we have a rota where we are split into teams, each team has three people in it and rotate though the different jobs. I have to learn how that steak was cooked.

After dinner we always have a chat from the guides about the countries we are going into so this one was all about South Africa. Justin, the guide, gave us a quick breeze through the history of SA and the economy, Nelson Mandela etc. and then handed over to Dennis, our driver. Dennis grew up in South Africa through the apartheid era and it was so interesting to hear firsthand about what it was really like and how the uprising happened. As a black man he was not allowed to visit friends and stay overnight without permission from the police who wanted to know what he was doing there and everything they would be talking about. He wasn't allowed a passport and had to go to the police to get travel documents just to cross a county border. It was also interesting to learn about Nelson

Mandela, apparently when he was first voted into power a lot of white people fled fearing repercussions from the black people in revenge for the years of segregation, but Nelson wasn't like that. He invited all of those people back in, saying it is a fresh start, we are a rainbow nation and everyone is welcome to be equal without fear. Having spent 27 years in prison to come out, into power and be that forgiving of years of torment and abuse is just something else. I don't believe there are many people in this world who would be able to do that. South Africa is still a long way from being fixed. Even if the leaders believe that, it doesn't mean the people do, you just hope that in time people will just learn to get along.

Currently we are about 100 km into our 550km journey today heading towards our campsite near Kruger National Park. We will be there for two days, at last a day without having to put that tent away! We have another game drive which hopefully we will see everything and I will have my right lens and it will be the right conditions, here's to hope!

Learnt on day 35;

1) I am pretty good at arsehole (the card game).

2) A lot, first hand, about apartheid and living as a black man in that time, shocking. There is an apartheid museum in Jo'berg but I won't get a chance to visit, it really is something I would like to learn more about in the future.

17. Day 38 - Flying Home

Day 38 - The long flight home

So here I am at the end of my trip, sat in Jo'berg airport (six hours early!) with a lovely coffee and just had a great breakfast - cured beef and fried halloumi, very different but nice. I cannot believe that the time has come for me to leave, I have seen so much, learnt so much and met so many great people. I hope I get to come back.

So I left the last entry as we were driving to Kruger, we arrived at the campsite about 3pm and were told that there were upgrades available. Until now every night we'd been staying in little tents that we had to put up and take down every day, often very early in the morning to leave in time for whatever we were doing. Being that we were staying at this place for two nights to upgrade to a dorm would have only been £10. When I looked at it the beds were plush, big and comfy and more importantly I didn't have to erect or destroy a tent again in the whole trip so as far I was concerned it was a no-brainer, upgrade accepted! Pretty much everyone in the group felt the same way and we quickly filled the dorm. There was only one who didn't so he was left in the campsite on his own, the only tent so we named the camping area. Garyville: population 1.

The first evening we arrived it was a bit cooler so there was no poolside chilling, we had dinner and then we had a cultural evening where a troop of local dancers came and performed traditional dance and song for us. It was done outside in Garyville and was very good. I really love the drum beats. At the end they grabbed us all up to boogie with them. I managed to borrow some pretty awesome goatskin wrist covers and danced a little solo with a Zulu warrior, much to the amusement of the rest of the group. In the photos I have seen he looks pretty manly, like he's on a hunt where as I look like I am wearing furry wrist covers and skipping around an imaginary maypole! Pretty camp you could say! It was a good night. After that we were given the good news that the game drive through Kruger leaves at 5:30am so we have to be at breakfast for 5, alarm set for 4:45am - that should be illegal!

So after an early night we had some breakfast and met up for our game drive in Kruger. It was slightly raining and another cooler day, something that we all appreciated. The drive itself was quite uneventful for the most part. We came across a giraffe pretty quickly but aside from that nothing else before breakfast. Well, loads of impalas, but they were everywhere and are pretty much just lion and leopard bait. We stopped for some breakfast and a look around the shop, I couldn't bring myself to buy anything, classic tourist pricing as you'd expect. Pretty soon after breakfast we heard on the radio that there were lions and cubs quite close by so we shot over there. Sadly by the time we were there they were gone so we missed them. I had seen loads of lions in Chobe, and touched them in Livingstone so I wasn't too fussed. They have all of the big five here and we were quite excited to finish ticking them off. In Chobe we managed to see four of them so we were all after a rhino spotting. Pretty soon after the lions' failure we heard radio chatter that there was a leopard in a tree not too far away, so off we chased again. You can always tell when you're close as there are a load of vehicles parked at the side of the road. This time we got our sighting. It was quite far away but this time I had the correct lens, conditions were not great, but I got a photo. The leopard had just made a kill and was wrapped around the tree while he was just chilling out, lying on his branch. I am always amazed at a leopard's tree climbing skills, especially getting the kills up the tree as well.

After the leopard we were just cruising along when one of the girls spotted a hyena at the side of the road, it was a good spot as, lying in the grass, it was well camouflaged. It looked in pretty bad shape, with a massive gash on the back of its head and various other marks. Given its position we all assumed that it had been hit by a car. Our guide was concerned it may have a broken back. He was just about to get out to check when the hyena stood up. With a better look at him you could see that it wasn't a car, he was probably trying to steal a lion's kill and was attacked but got away. As well as the massive gash on his back you could notice puncture wounds from teeth all over him. If he was hit by a car they would have called the vet out. They have vets who look after the animals when they have been hurt by any kind of human activity but when it is nature they just let it happen. I think it's the right thing to do too. Once up the hyena just trotted along the road next to us for about 200 metres before dipping off into the bushes, which was a great addition to the trip. I didn't even think I'd see a hyena. That was pretty much it before lunch, apart from loads more impalas and other lion buffet items. Due to the lack of sightings, by lunch we were all feeling a little down and worried what the afternoon would bring. We had lunch up on a rock which was high enough to see for miles, pretty spectacular views.

We started driving again, due to the time we were slowly heading back to the gate and once again there was some radio chatter, this time a confirmed sighting of an elephant, blah, seen loads of them, but also a possible rhino sighting.

Speeding up we quickly found the elephant, we also found a zebra family with a couple of babies but we needed rhinos. We sped off to the sighting and there right in front of us, two wild white rhinos side by side. They were close to the watering hole and walked straight past us to get to it. They laid in the water and just relaxed. It was quite fun because all the hippos noticed and started swimming over, we thought there was going to be a fight. Apparently they don't fight though just try to intimidate each other. Even without a fight, a hippo rhino standoff was something special to see. On the other side there were impalas fighting zebras grazing and drinking, all it needed to have been perfect was a lion to come through and make a kill, sadly that didn't happen but an amazing end to a pretty good game drive and we managed to complete the big five sightings. In the evening our guides, Dennis and Justin, cooked us a traditional African meal consisting of a beef stew with ulaki (Kenyan name, the maize dough has a different name in every country), spinach cooked with tomatoes and onion and pumpkin leaves cooked in peanut butter. That last one sounds weird but was amazing. The evening was another chilled one in the bar before heading to bed.

In the morning we were up at 7 for a 7:30am departure to Jo'Berg. It is quite sad that at the moment 7:30am is a lie-in! The drive was pretty standard, stopped for lunch at a roadside service station. Best toilets in Africa by a long way, had a panoramic window overlooking African plains with buffalo grazing and ostriches running. Sadly I don't always take my camera to the toilet with me so I have no photos of that. The drive was amazingly scenic and we pretty much played cards the whole way there, people dipped in and out of the game but I managed to hold my record of playing every single game that was played on the bus. We arrived at the hostel around 3pm, checked into the dorm and then followed the standard procedure of chilling by the pool with a couple of beers. I am going to miss this when I get back . . . to winter! In the evening we went out to dinner as a group with a few cocktails before heading back to crash. Some of our group left at this point so we said our goodbyes and swapped all our Facebook details etc.

This morning I shared a taxi with three other girls heading to the airport. This made it the easiest and cheapest way, but sadly I arrived six hours early so two and a half hours later here I am still waiting to check in. Hopefully not much longer before I am on my way for a brief stop in Doha and then on to jolly old England. I said final goodbyes to my Aussie friends and now here I sit, alone, just waiting.

What I learnt on my trip home;

1) Only one bit of advice here that I feel you need to know, Doha is a dry airport. Now I am a firm believer that beer always tastes better in airports...just not Doha, no matter how many times you walk up and down you will not find a bar. I did a lot of laps.

18. Final Thoughts

Final thoughts

It's been a few days now since I arrived home and how does it all feel now? Well I made it home safe and I can say I truly had an amazing time. The people I met every step of the way are what made the trip. From Charles in Nairobi, all the guys in Iringa and then the fun on the safari it has been amazing. I jokingly gave some of the Aussie girls a couple of spare passport photos of me as a leaving present and now pictures are appearing of me in Cape Town and Bondi Beach - all great fun! I never really met many Australians I liked before but this trip has opened my eyes and I now fancy a trip down under. I have learnt that the guys still volunteering in Iringa have managed to get seven of the kids from the Upendo orphanage into school, sponsored by themselves and various families from home. One of them is little Ali who I loved so much so that is some of the best news. It sounds like things in Iringa are coming along. I really hope my short time there has helped even if just a little bit. The volunteers are already achieving an amazing effect in the short time that it has been running and things will only get better. I hope in the future I can go back, but whether I will or not is still to be seen as there is so much of the world out there waiting for me to discover it. What I have learnt travelling through Africa alone in five weeks is more than I can ever imagined and I hope that this experience has made me a better person. I would love to do some more volunteering - and travelling - in the future, I have been looking at a project in Cambodia..........wait and see!

19. All the Travel Advice You will Ever Need

To Finish

I hope you enjoyed reading about my experience, if you are planning to go here is just a summary of some of the main points that I learnt along the way which I really hope will help you with your trip

1) Do not drink too much the day before you fly.
2) Get your jabs sorted in plenty of time.
3) Never leave your wallet behind at an airport scanner when you have lost your voice. In fact don't leave it behind at all.
4) Visas can be bought at the airport, just check on the Kenyan Embassy website which one will be best for you and don't forget about the multiple entry option, could save you a lot of money.
5) Ensure you get a price from the taxi driver before you get into the car and barter barter barter, you can get the price down as there are lots of taxis wanting your business.
6) Not everyone who approaches you in the street is a crook, guides are a great way to see the local area and learn as you go, I guess you just have to use your intuition to choose the right one or I can highly recommend going to www.trekkingkenya.com to track down Charles and arrange a meeting point before you leave.
7) Buy your tickets for onward travel as early as possible.
8) Tuk tuks are awesome.

9) You will spend more money than you think!

10) Culture shock is a bitch, which is what I am putting my fear for the first few days down to.

11) Take a universal plug if you want to keep your pants kind of clean.

12) If you have to exchange money at a border make sure you negotiate and don't change too much.

13) Inside a bus station if you need help look to ask the people loading the buses but beware some of them will tell you to get on their bus and charge you for another ticket so stay smart.

14) Learn a few words of the local language so you can initiate some interactions.

15) Remember to work out how much you need to spend on visas throughout your trip and keep the money in dollars as it is the only payment they will accept, keep cash with you at all times!

16) You have to make your own choice about whether you take things to throw out to kids from the train, but make sure you take plenty or expect some fights!

17) Stay in hostels if you are travelling alone and want to meet people. One of the guys I met gave me the advice that if you are alone in a hostel, grab a beer, find the largest group and just ask if they mind if you join them. This way there will be no pressure on you to talk, you can just listen, learn names, see what they are like, join in if you want but above all as it was the largest group the next day most people around the hostel will know your face and say hello to you. Good advice and it works.

18) Do the Devils pool trip. Make sure you book it before you go to the Victoria Falls park.
19) Have an amazing time, meet some amazing people, learn stuff, buy stuff, travel safe, be smart, trust, be trustworthy, live your life.

18994228R00059

Printed in Poland
by Amazon Fulfillment
Poland Sp. z o.o., Wrocław